A Comprehensive Course in
LIBRARY AND INFORMATION SCIENCE
(Objective Type Questions for UGC- NET/JRF, SLET, PSC, UPSC and Other Competitive Examinations)

A Comprehensive Course in LIBRARY AND INFORMATION SCIENCE

(Objective Type Questions for UGC-NET/JRF, SLET, PSC, UPSC and Other Competitive Examinations)

By

NASIRUDHEEN. T

University of Calicut

Ess Ess Publications

New Delhi

A Comprehensive Course in Library and Information Science
{Objective Type Questions for UGC-NET/JRF, SLET, PSC, UPSC & Other Competitive Examinations}

ISBN: 978-81-7000-662-6

Ess Ess
Rs.700/-

First Published 2012

Published by:
Ess Ess Publications
4831/24, Ansari Road,
Darya Ganj,
New Delhi-110 002.
INDIA
Phones: 23260807, 41563444
Fax: 41563334
E-mail: info@essessreference.com
www.essessreference.com

Cover Design by *Patch Creative Unit*

Printed and bound in India at Salasar Imaging Systems.

CONTENTS

PART 2 : GENERAL QUESTIONS-FIELD/SUBJECT WISE

FOREWORD

Library and Information science has gained fast growth and development in its theory and application. The subject has been taught in graduate, post graduate and doctoral levels in India and abroad. As a field of application, library and information profession has got dignified status in academic and corporate institutions.

Library and information science course imparts certain technical skills, professional attitude and strong knowledge about knowledge acquisition, organization and dissemination. For employment in LIS profession, sharp and in-depth understanding of the subject is a must. In this highly competitive world, only fittest can survive. This book aims to make aspirants fit for all competitive examinations.

The book has been organized in three parts, first part entitled- General awareness is a ready reference part for getting any information in LIS field. The second part deals with multiple choice questions and answers of six major fields in LIS, and the third part has been included solved question papers of seven recent competitive examinations .I wish readers success in their competitive examinations and career.

Dr. V Jalaja

Former Head,

Department of Library and Information Science,

University of Calicut

Part-1 : General Awareness

1. Historical Events in LIS

1759	British Museum act was passed
1800	Library of Congress (LC) was founded
1829	First edition of Encyclopedia Americana
1835	Calcutta public library was setup
1836	Calcutta public library opened to public
1837	C.A Cutter was born
1848	Library legislation started in USA
1850	Library act was passed in England
1851	Dewey was born
1857	First edition of Oxford English Dictionary
1867	First copyright act
1870	Copyright law was passed in USA
1870	H.E Bliss was born
1876	ALA was founded
1876	American Library Association was formed
1876	First edition of DDC
1877	Library Association (UK) was formed
1882	Hunter commission was appointed
1887	First library science school started at Columbia University by Dewey
1891	Cutter' Expansive Classification
1892	Ranganathan was born
1903	Calcutta public library was changed as Imperial library
1907	Chemical Abstract was published firstly
1911	W Borden from America came India for revival of public library systems I India
1915	Adams report came out
1915	Dickinson came India

1917	Sadler commission was set up
1924	Kenyon committee was appointed in UK
1924	Ranganathan went to England for education
1926	Biological Abstract was started
1926	Association of special libraries (ASLIB) was formed
1927	Kenyon committee submitted
1928	Five laws of library science was enunciated by Ranganathan
1930	All Asia educational conference held at Banaras
1931	Five Laws of Library science was first published
1933	Colon Classification (CC) by SR.Ranganathan was published
1933	First All India library conference held at Calcutta
1938	ALA adopted a professional ethical code
1947	Calcutta public library was setup
1950	British National Bibliography (BNB) was first published
1950	word ' information retrieval ' was first used
1951	Library research circle (LRC) was founded by SR.Ranganathan
1952	Classification research group (CRG) was formed
1952	Indian National scientific documentation centre (INSDOC) was formed
1952	Mudaliyar commission was set up
1953	University grants commission (UGC) was set up

1954	Delivery of book act was passed
1956	Amendment of delivery of books act was passed
1957	Computer was firstly used in India by ISI Calcutta
1957	First PhD in library science has been awarded to B Krishna Rao by Delhi University
1957	IAEA was established
1957	Indian National Bibliography (INB) was first published
1957	Ranganathan committee was setup
1957	word 'thesaurus' was first used
1958	Degree course in library science started at Aligarh Muslim University
1958	Scientific Information Bureau (SIB-presently DESIDOC)
1959	British museum opened for public
1960	Science Citation Index was started
1960	Word ' information' was firstly used
1962	DRTC was formed
1965	Indian Science Abstract was started publication
1966	Machine readable catalogue (MARC) came out
1967	AACR-1 came out
1967	Wadia committee was setup
1968	Association scientific information dissemination centre (ASIDIC) was formed
1970	European association of scientific information dissemination centre (EUSIDIC) was formed

1970	INIS started
1970	DESIDOC was established
1971	SENDOC was established
1972	British library Act was passed
1972	Raja Ram Mohan Roy Library foundation (RRLF) was founded at Calcutta
1972	ISBN was started in the world
1972	Ranganathan was died
1974	AGRIS started
1975	UNESCO PGI programs started
1977	BLAISE started
1977	NICNET started
1978	AACR-2 came out
1983	Technology policy of Govt. of India was formed
1985	CD-ROM was developed
1985	Copyright act was passed
1985	Govt. of India appointed committee on National policy on library & information system
1985	ISBN was started in India
1986	ERNET started
1986	National book policy came out
1986	National policy on education was passed in India
1989	International society for Knowledge organization was formed
1989	MS-Office was developed
1994	UNESCO public library manifesto came out
2001	Wikipedia was developed

2004	Google was developed
2005	National Knowledge Commission
2005	Right to information Act
2007	ISBN became in the present form (13 digits)
2009	Right to Education Act was passed in India
2011	23rd Edition of DDC was published.

2. Abbreviations

A

AA Code	Anglo American Code
AACR	Anglo American Cataloguing Rules
ABGILA	Annals Bulletin Grandhalya of Indian Library Association
ABN	Australian Bibliographic Network
ADONIS	Article Delivery over Network Information System
AEC	Atomic Energy Commission
AGRIS	Agricultural Information System
AIU	Association of Indian Universities
ALA	American Library Association
ALU	Arithmetic and Logic Unit
AMIC	Asian Mass communication Information Centre
ANN	Asia-pacific News Network
ANSI	American National Standard Institute
APUPA	Alien Penumbral Umbrel Penumbral Alien
ARPANET	Advanced Research Project Network
ASCII	American Standard Code for Information Interchange

ASIDIC	Association of Scientific Information Dissemination Centre.
ASLIB	Association of Special Libraries & Information Bureau
AVI	Audio Video Interleave

B

BARC	Bhabha Atomic Research Centre
BASDOC	Bangladesh national Scientific Documentation Centre
BASIC	Beginners all Purpose Symbolic Instruction Code
BHEL Network	Bharat Heavy Electrical, Ltd. Network
BIS	Bureau of Indian Standards
BLA	British library association
BLAISE	British Library Automated Information Services (UK)
BNB	British national bibliography
BONET	Bombay Library Network
BPS	Bits per Second
BRAISE	British Automated Information Service
BSO	Broad System of Ordering

C

CALIBNET	Calcutta Library Network
CALIS	China Academic Library & Information System
CAPS	Content, Abstract and Photocopy Service
CAS	Current Awareness Service
CAS	Chemical Abstracting Service
CC	Colon Classification

CCC	Classified Catalogue Code
CCF	Common Communication Language
CCL	Common Command Language
CD-ROM	Compact Disc Read only Memory
CDS/ISIS	Computerized Documentation System/ Integrated sets of Information system.
CIP	Cataloguing in Publication
COMLA	Commonwealth Library Association
COMPASS	Computer Aided Subject System
CRDI	Central Drug Research Institute
CSIR	Council of Scientific and Industrial Research
CURL	Consortium for University Libraries

D

DBMS	Database Management System
DDC	Dewey Decimal Classification
DDL	Data Definition Language
DEC	Data Evaluation Centre
DESIDOC	Defense, science Information and Documentation Centre.
DEVSIS	Development Science Information System
DML	Data Manipulation Language
DOI	Digital Object Identifier
DVD	Digital Video Disc

E

EARN	European Academic Research Network
ERNET	Education and Research Network

EUSIDIC	European association of scientific information dissemination centre.

F

FDT	Field Definition Table (in CDS/ISIS)
FID	International Federation for Information and Documentation.
FORSA	Forum for Resource Sharing in Astronomy and Astrophysics.
FORTRAN	Formulae Translation
FST	Field Selection Table

G

GIF	Graphic Interchange Format
GOC	Good Office Committee
GPSS	Gateway packet Switching Service

H

HELINET	Health Science Library and Information Networks
HRD	Human Resource Development
HRM	Human Resource Management
HTML	Hypertext Markup Language
HTTP	Hypertext Transfer Protocol

I

IAEA	International Atomic Energy Agency
IALL	International Association of Law Libraries
IASLIC	Indian association of special libraries & Information Centres.
IATLIS	Indian association of Teachers in Library & Information Science

IBM	International Business Machine
ICAR	Indian Council of Agricultural Research
ICAR	Indian Council of Agricultural Research
ICHR	Indian Council of Historic Research
ICMR	Indian Council of Medical Research
ICSSR	Indian Council of Social Science Research
IDSA	Institute of Defense Studies and Analysis (New Delhi)
IFIS	International Food Information Service
IFLA	International Federation of Library Associations & institutions.
ILA	Indian Library Association
ILL	Inter Library Loan
ILSA	Indian Library Science Abstract
IMO	Information Market Observation
INB	Indian national bibliography
INDEST	Indian National Digital Library in Science and Technology.
INFLIBNET	Information and Library Network
INIS	International Nuclear Information System
INSDOC	Indian National Scientific Documentation Centre
ISBD	International Standard Bibliographic Description
ISBD (CM)	International Standard Bibliographic Description (Cartographic Material).
ISBD (G)	International Standard Bibliographic

	Description (General).
ISBD (M)	International Standard Bibliographic Description (Monographs).
ISBD (NBM)	International Standard Bibliographic Description (Non-Book Material).
ISBD(S)	International Standard Bibliographic Description (Serial).
ISBN	International Standard Book Number
ISCII	Indian Standard Code for Information Interchange
ISDN	Integrated Service Digital Network
ISDS	International Serials Data System
ISI	Indian Standard Institute
ISO	International Standard Organization
ISRO	Indian Space Research Organization
ISRS	Information Storage and Retrieval System
ISSN	International Standard Serial Number
ITES	Information Technology Enabled Service
ITIB	Industrial and Technological Information Bank

J

JANET	Joint Academic Network
JPEG	Joint Photographic Expert Group

K

KWIC	Key Word in Context
KWOC	Key Word Out of Context

L

LA	Library Association
LAA	Library Association of Australia
LAN	Local Area Network
LCC	Library of Congress Classification
LCHS	Library of Congress Subject Headings
LIBRIS	Library Information System (Stock home)
LISA	Library and Information science abstract
LITA	Library and Information Technology Association (Chicago).
LOCIS	Library of Congress Information System
LSI	Large Scale Integration

M

MARC	Machine Readable Catalogue
MBO	Management by Objective
MEDLARS	Medical Literature Analysis and Retrieval System
MEDLINE	Medical Library Network
MICR	Magnetic Ink Character Recorder
MILNET	Military Network
MIS	Management information systems
MLA	Medical Library Association
MPEG	Motion Pictures Expert Group

N

NACLIN	National Convention on knowledge, Library and -Information Networking.

NAI	National Archives of India
NAL	National Aeronautical Laboratory
NAPC	National Program for Acquisition and Cataloguing
NAPLIS	National policy on library & information system
NASA	National Aeronautical Space Agency
NASSDOC	National Social Science Documentation Centre
NASSIC	National Social Science Information Centre (Vadodara).
NATIS	National Information System
NBT	National Book Trust
NCCP	National Coordinated Cataloguing Program
NCSI	National Centre for Science Information (Bangalore)
NIC	National Informatics Centre
NICNET	National Informatics Centre Network
NII	National Institute of Immunology (New Delhi)
NISIET	National Institute of Small Industry Extension Training (Hyderabad).
NISSAT	National information system for science & technology
NIXI	National Internet Exchange of India.
NLM	National Library of Medicine (USA)
NML	National Medical Library (New Delhi)
NTC	National Translation Centre (Chicago)
NTIS	National Technical Information Service (USA)

NUCSSI	National Union Catalogue of Scientific Serials In India

O

OCLC	Online Computer Library Centre
OCR	Optical Character Recognition
OECD	Organisation for Economic Cooperation and Development.
OLAS	Online Acquisition System
OPAC	Online public access catalogue

P

PC	Personal Computer
PDF	Portable Document Format
PDNs	Public Data Networks
PERT	Program Evaluation Review Technique
PGI	General Information Program
PIS	Patent Information System
PNG	Portable Network Graphics
POPIN	Population Information Network
POSDCORB	Planning, organizing, directing, coordinating, reporting, and budgeting.
PPBS	Planning Programming Budgeting System
PPP	Point to Point Protocol
PRECIS	Preserved Context Indexing System
PROM	Programmable Read only Memory
PTLA	Publishers Trade List Annual

R

RAILNET	Computer Network for Railway

RAM	Random Access Memory
RAMP	Records and Archives Management Program
RET Act	Right to Education Act
RFID	Radio Frequency Identification Technology
RLIN	Research Libraries and Information Network
ROM	Read Only Memory
RTI Act	Right to Information Act

S

SANDOC	Small Enterprises National Documentation Centre
SBDN	Satellite Based Data Network
SCI	Scientific Citation Index
SDI	Selective dissemination of Information
SEAMIC	South-East Asian Medical Information Centre
SENDOC	Small Enterprises National Documentation Centre
SHE	Subject Heading for Engineering
SIRNET	Scientific and Industrial Research Network
SLIP	Serial Line Internet Protocol
SONET	Synchronous Optical Network
SPC	Stored Program Control
SPIN	Special Interest Network
SQL	Structured Query Language
SSCI	Social Science Citation Index
STAIRS	Storage & information retrieval system

T

TCP/IP	Transmission Control Protocol / Internet Protocol
TDNs	Terrestrial Data Networks
TELEX	Tele-printer Exchange
TIB	Technology Information Bank
TIFF	Tagged Image File Format
TIFR	Tata Institute of Fundamental Research
TIPS	Technology Information Pilot System
TIS	Trade Information Service
TOP	Technical and Office Protocol
TQM	Total quality management
TRC	Technology Research Centre

U

UAP	Universal Availability of Publication
UDC	Universal Decimal Classification
UIN	User Identification Number
UNESCO	United Nations Educational Scientific and Cultural Organisation.
UNISIST	United Nations Information System in Science and Technology.
UNIVAC	Universal Automatic Computer
URL	Uniform Resource Locator
UTLAS	University of Toronto Library Automation System

V

VDU	Visual Display Unit
VGA	Video Graphic Adapter

VLSI	Very Large Scale Integration
W	
WAN	Wide Area Network
WAPIS	Water and Power Information System
WLN	Western Library Network
WLS	Western Library Network
WLSP	World List of Scientific Periodicals
WORM	Write Once Read Many times
WPI	World Patent Index
WTI	World Translation Index
WWW	World Wide Web
X	
XML	Extensible Markup Language
XNS	Xerox Network System
Z	
ZBB	Zero Based Budgeting

3. Nick Name

Dewey of Japan	Fujio
Father of Bibliography	Corard Genser
Father of encyclopedia	Aristotle
Father of Indian Library science	S.R Ranganathan
Father of scientific management	F.W Taylor
Grammarian of Library classification	Berwick Sayers
Prince of biographers	James Boswell
Ranganathan of Pakistan	Dr.Khursheed

4. Books & Authors

A better India, a better world	N.R. Narayana Moorthy
Art of making catalogues.	Crestadoro
Canon of classification.	W.C.B Sayers
Classification, theories and practical.	E.C Richardson
Computer and Common sense.	Mortimer Taub
Computer Liberation and Dream Machine.	Ted Nelson
Documentation and Information.	Guha
Five laws of library science.	S.R Ranganathan
Foundations of education for librarianship.	J.H Shera
Grammar of classification.	W.C.B Sayers
Hints on library administration.	R.L Bhatia
History of catalogue and cataloguing methods.	D.M Noris
How to judge books.	Edwin L Shuman
Librarian's glossary of terms.	M.L.M Harrod
Little Science Big Science.	Deric De Solla Price
Manual of library economy.	J.D Brown
National library of India: a critical study.	P.N Kaula
Organisation of knowledge & the system - of science.	H.E Bliss
Organisation of knowledge in libraries and subject Approach to books.	H.E Bliss

Philosophy of user education.	Girija Kumar
Principles of book classification.	E.W Hulme
Production & distribution of Knowledge in US.	Fritz Machulp
Prolegomena to library classification	S.R Ranganathan
Punjab library primer	Asa Don Dickinson
Putting knowledge to work	Pauline Atherton
Reader in comparative librarianship	D.J Foskett
Rules for dictionary catalogue	C.A Cutter
Studies in co-ordinate indexing	Mortimer Taub
The Art of computer programming	Donald Neuth
Towards paperless information systems	Lancaster
Traits De Documentation	Paul Autlet

5. First in Library Science

First All India Conference of Librarians	Lahore-1918
First Classificationist	E.C Richardson
First director of DRTC	S.R Ranganthan
First Indian state, which passed library act	Tamilnadu
First Indian University PG course in Library Science.	Delhi University

First Indian University started degree course in Library science.	Aligarh Muslim University
First Indian University started diploma course in Library science.	University of Madras
First journal of library science	Library Journal" by Dewey
First librarian of imperial library- Calcutta	John Macfarlane
First librarian of National Library-Calcutta	B.S Kesavan
First library association formed in India	Andra desa library association (1914).
First library journal in India	Modern Librarian-1935
First library journal published in India	Library miscellany
First library science book written by an Indian.	Hints of library administration by B.H Mehta.
First National Research Professor in library Science appointed by Govt. of India	S.R Ranganthan
First person who used "thesaurus" in Information Retrieval.	Helen Brownson
First PhD. Holder in Library science in India.	D.B Krishna Rao
First president of IFLA.	Isaac Colijn (the then Swedish national librarian)

First president of the Library Association	J.Winter Jones
First school of library science started at	Columbia University
First school of library science started by	Melvil Dewey
First school of library science started on	1887
First 'emeritus fellow' professor of Library and Information science appointed by UGC.	P.N Kaula
First encyclopedia in the world	Historia Naturalis
First chairman of UGC	C.D Deshmugh
First president of COMLA	Kenneth C Harrison

6. Publications & Publishers

American book of publishing record	R.R Bowker -New York
Bibliography on India in 2000	NASSDOC
Book Review Digest	H.W Wilson- New York
Books in Print	R.R Bowker -New York
Cumulative book index	H.W Wilson- New York
Current Biography	H.W Wilson- New York
Data India	PTI
Dictionary of National Bibliography	University Press, London.
Encyclopedia of Americana	Grolier
Encyclopedia of Library Science	Marcel Decker

Index Translationum	UNESCO
Indian book Industry	Sterling Publishers- New Delhi
Indian Library Science Abstract	IASLIC
Indian National bibliography	Central reference library Calcutta
Indian Science abstract	NISCAIR
International Who is who	Europa
Journal of Librarianship	The Library Association
Library Literature	H.W Wilson- New York
Library Trend	University of Illinois
New Encyclopaedia Britannica	Britannica, Inc, Chicago
Publishers weekly	R.R Bowker- New York
Roster of Indian Scientific & Technical Translator.	NISCAIR
Science Citation Index	Institute of Scientific Information, Philadelphia
Summary of World Broadcast	BBC
Translationum Indicorum	National Library, Calcutta
Universities Handbook	Association of Indian - Universities
University News	Association of Indian Universities
World of Learning	Europa, London
World Tables	World Bank

7. Terms - Coined /Developed By

Bespeaking (reservation)	SR.Ranganathan
Bibliography	Louis Jaconde saint Charles
Bibliometrics	Alan Prichard
Cyber Space	William Gibson
Global Village	Marshel Mc Luhan
Hypertext	Ted Nelson
Informatics	Chernyi & Gilyarevarkii
Information retrieval	Calvine Moores
Initiation of readers	SR.Ranganathan
Librametry	SR.Ranganathan
Library science	SR.Ranganathan
MBO	Peter Drucker
Pre-natal cataloguing	SR.Ranganathan
Paperless society	F.W Lancaster
Technological	Gate keepers Derik Austin
Thesaurus	Helen Brownson
TQM	Deming & Juran

8. Word & Origin

Bibliography	Greek word
Book	German word
Catalogue	Greek word
Classification	Latin word
Computer	Latin word
Encyclopedia	Greek word
Libra	Latin word
Mnemonics	Latin word
Thesaurus	Greek word
Vocabulary	Latin word

9. Observations

Librarian's Day	August 12
National News paper Day	January-29
National library week	November 14th -20th
World Animation Day	October-28
World Book Day	April-23
World communication Day	November-05
World Literacy Day	September-05

10. Related with

Andra Crestdro	Keyword Indexing
Calvin Moores	Literature search
Derik Austine	PRECIS
E.W Hulme	Principles of literary warrant
G. Bhattacharyya	POPSI
Gordon Foster	ISBN
HP Luhn	KWIC
Neena E Brown	Browny charging system
Patricia B Knap	User Education
Peter phyr	Zero based budgeting system
S.R Ranganathan	Three card system
Thomas Bray	Monastic libraries

11. Conferences / Seminars

Conference/Seminar & Year	Place
Berne Convention for the protection of literary and artistic work -1886	Berne

First international Conference on bibliography- 1895	Brussels
All Asia educational conference-1930	Banaras
First All India Library conference-1933	Calcutta
Universal Copyright Convention-1952	Geneva
First international study conference on Classification research (ISCCR)- 1957	Dorking(UK)
International conference on scientific information-1958	Washington
International conference on cataloguing principles-1961	Paris
Regional seminar on development of national Library in Asia & Pacific-1964	Manila
Second ISCCR-1964	Denmark
International meeting of cataloguing experts-1969	Copenhagen
Third international conference on classification Research-1975	Bombay
First International conference on library User education-1979	Cambridge
Fourth ISCCR-1982	Germany
First conference of International Federation of Classification Societies (at Aacher) -1987	Germany
Fifth ISCCR-1991	Toronto
Sixth ISCCR-1997	London

12. Acts / Commissions

Act/Commission	Year
Hunter commission	1882
Indian University commission	1902

Adams committee (for public libraries)	1915
Sadler commission	1917
Kenyon committee (for public libraries)	1924
Kenyon committee report (for public libraries)	1927
Mc Clovin committee (for public libraries)	1941
Imperial Library Act	1948
Radhakrishna commission/university education commission	1948
Mudaliyar commission /secondary education commission	1953
University Grants Commission	1953
Delivery of books and newspaper act	1954
Delivery of books and newspaper act (Revision)	1956
Robert Committee (for public libraries)	1957
Indian copyright act	1957
Ranganathan Committee (Library Committee)	1957
Advisory Committee (Sinha Committee)	1958
Kothari Commission	1964
Khuda baksh oriental public library act	1969
Elementary education act	1970
Patent Act, India	1970
Mehrotra committee (for pay revision & profl.development)	1983
Asiatic society act	1986
New Education Policy	1986
WIPO Copyright Act	1996
Rastogi Committee (for pay revision)	1997
Information Technology Act	2000
Right to Information Act	2005
Right to Education Act	2009

13. Quotations/Wordings

Quotations/Wordings	By
A room without book is like a body without a soul.	Marcus Tullus Cicero
A truly great library contain something in it to Offend everyone.	Jo Godwin
A university is a group of buildings gathered around library.	Shelby Foote
Catalogue is a list of books.	C.A Cutter
Classification is arranging of things according to likeness and unlikeness.	Margaret Mann
Classification is the arrangements of books on shelves or description of them in the manner which is most helpful to those who read.	W.C Berwick Sayers
Classification is the systematic arrangement of books on shelves.	Arthur Maltby
Classification is the translation of the name of the subject of a book into preferred artificial language of ordinal numbers.	Ranganathan
Classification made ape man.	E.C Richardson-
Dissemination Knowledge is one of the corner stone of Civilization.	John F Budh
Foundation of library is books, and foundation of	

librarianship is classification.	Berwick Sayers
He is wise who knows the source of knowledge- where it is written and where it is to be found.	AA Hodge
I would never read the book if it were possible to talk half an hour with the man who wrote it.	Thomas Woodrow Wilson.
In a metaphorical sense, we are moving from a Ptolemaic world with the library at the centre to a Copernican one with Information at the centre and library as one of its planets.	Robert S Taylor
Information is product & process.	J Martin
Information is the currency of democracy	Thomas Jefferson
Nothing helps memory so much as order and classification.	John Stuart -Blackie
Once you learn to read, you will be for ever free.	Frederic Douglas
Reading is to the mind what exercise is to body	Richard Steele
Some books are to be tasted, others are to be swallowed. and some to be chewed and digested.	Fracis Bacon

The eternal conflict of good and the best with bad and the worst is on	Melvil Dewey
The librarian must be the librarian militant before he Can be the librarian triumphant.	Melvil Dewey
The man who doesn't read good books, has no advantage over the man who cannot read them.	Mark Twain
There is far greater peril in buying knowledge, than in buying meat and drink.	Plato
To read without reflecting is like eating without digesting.	Edmund Barke
When I get a little money, I buy books and if any is left I buy food and cloths.	Desideruis -Erasmus
Where there is wisdom, we lost in knowledge	T.S Eliot
Wisdom begins with wonder	Socrates

14. 5 Laws by S.R Ranganathan

1st Law	Books are for use
2nd Law	Every reader his/ her book
3rd Law	Every book its reader
4th Law	To save the time of the reader
5th Law	Library is a growing organism

15. Bibliometric Laws

Lotka's law of scientific productivity (1926)

Bradford's law of scattering (1934)

Zip's law of word occurrence (1949)

16. Book Selection Principles

Drury's Principle (1930) : "To provide the right book to the right reader at the right time".

Dewey's Principle : "The best reading for the largest at the least cost".

Mclovins Principle (1925) : "Books in themselves are nothing, they have no more meaning than the white paper upon which they are printed, until they are made serviceable by demand".

Ranganathan's principle: 1931: 5 laws of library science

17. Terms and storage capacity

1 Nibble	4 Bits
1 Byte	8 Bits
1 KB (Kilo Byte)	1024 Byte
1 MB (Mega Byte)	1024 KB
1 GB (Gega Byte)	1024 MB
1 TB (Tera Byte)	1024 GB

18. Decimal – Binary

Decimal	Binary
1	01
2	10
3	11

4	100
5	101
6	110
7	111
8	1000
9	1001
10	1010
11	1011
12	1100
13	1101
14	1110
15	1111

19. Cataloguing Codes

Code	Year
British Museum Cataloguing Code/Antony Panizzy Code	1841
Jewett's rules	1852
Cutter's rules	1876
AA Code	1908
CCC	1934
ALA rule	1941
AACR-1	1967
AACR-2	1978

20. Subject Indexing Models

Model	Example
Authority lists based subject indexing Model.	Library of Congress subject -Headings, Sears list of subject headings
Pre-co-ordinate Indexing Model	Chain procedure, PRECIS, POPSI
Post Co-ordinate Indexing Model	Uniterm Indexing
Key word based indexing model	KWIC, KWAC, and KWOC

21. Institutions and Location

Institutions / Organization	Location
British library	London
Classification Research Group (CRG)	London
Documentation Research & Training Centre (DRTC)	Bangalore
Indian office library	London
International Atomic Energy Agency (IAEA)	Vienna
International society for Knowledge Organisation (ISKO)	Frankfurt (Germany)
Library Research Circle (LRC)	New Delhi
National library of blind & physical handicapped	Dehradun
Raja Ram Mohan Roy Library Foundation (RRLF)	Calcutta
School of librarianship	London

22. National Research Institutes

Institute	Place
Bhabha Atomic Research Centre	Mumbai
Central Building Research Institute	Roorkie (UP)
Central Drug research Institute	Lucknow
Central Food & Technological Research Institute	Mysore
Central Land Capture Fisheries Research Institute	Barrackporel (WB)
Central Leather research Institute	Madras
Central Machine tool Institute	Bangalore
Central Marine Research Institute	Kochi
Central Plantation Research Institute	Kasargode (Kerala)
Central Power Research Institute	Bangalore
Centre for Development Studies	Thiruvanant-apuram
Centre for Earth Science Studies	Thiruvanant-apuram
Indian Institute of Plasma Research	Ahmedadabad
Indian Institute of Pulse Research	Kanpur
Indian Institute of vegetable Research	Varanasi (UP)
Institute for Crystallography & Biophysics	Madras
Institute for Textile industry	Ahmedadabad
Jawaharlal Nehru Centre for Advanced Research	Bangalore
National Botanical Research Institute	Lucknow

National Chemical Laboratory	Pune
National Forest Research Institute	Dehradun
National Metallurgical Laboratory	New Delhi
National Physical Laboratory	New Delhi
National Research Centre for Agro forestry	Jhansi (UP)
Tata Institute of Fundamental Research	Mumbai

23. Library Associations

Library Associations	Year of Establishment
International	
ASLIB	1924
Association of Christian Libraries	1957
ALA- Chicago	1876
Canadian Library Association	1946
IFLA	1927
LA- UK	1877
Special Library Association (SLA)	1909
National	
All India College library association	1966
Andra Desa Library Association	1914
Baroda Library Association	1910
Bengal Library Association	1927
BLA (Bengal Library Association)	1925
BOSLA (Bombay Science Library Association)	1970
Delhi Library Association	1953

Govt. of India library association	1933
IASLIC- Calcutta	1955
IATLIS	1970
Indian Library Association	1933
Indian Library Association	1933
KLA (Kerala Library Association)	1972
Madras Library Association	1927
RRLF (Rajaram Mohonroy Library Foundation)	1972

24. Information Systems

International

CAS	Chemical Abstracts Service	1907
MEDLARS	Medical Literature Analysis & Retrieval System	1964
INSPEC		1967
BIOSIS		1969
INIS	International Nuclear Information system (Vienna)	1970
INFOTERRA	Global Environmental Information Network (Nairobi)	1972
UNISIST	World Science Information System (Paris)	1972
ISDS	International Serial Data Systems (Paris)	1973
DEVSIS	Development Science Information System (Canada)	1974
AGRIS	International Information System for Agriculture (Rome)	1974
ASINFO		1983

National

NIC	National Informatics Centre	1975
NISSAT	National Information System for Science& Technology	1977
ENVIS	Environment Information System	1982
BITS	Biotechnology Information System	1987

25. Documentation Centres

Centre	Head Quarters	Year
INSDOC	New Delhi (NISCAIRE)	1952
NASSDOC	New Delhi	1969
SENDOC	Hyderabad	1971
DESIDOC(SIB)	New Delhi	1958
DRTC	Bangalore	1962

26. Exchange Formats

Name	Developed By	Year
MARC	LC	1965
UNIMARC	IFLA	1977
CCF	UNESCO	1984

27. Indexing techniques

Pre co-ordinate	Developer	Year
Dictionary catalogue	C.A Cutter	1876
Systematic indexing	Kaiser	1911
Chain Indexing	Ranganathan	1934
PRECIS	Derik Austin	1974

Relational Indexing	Farradane	1980
POPSI	Bhattacharyya	1979
Post co-ordinate		
Uniterm Indexing	Eugene Garfield	1953
KWIC	HP Luhn	1959

28. Library Networks

Name	Full form	Year
ADINET	Ahemedabad Library Network	1993
BALNET	Bangalore Library Network	1995
CALIBNET	Calcutta Library Network	1993
DELNET	Delhi Library Network	1988
ERNET	Education and Research Network	1986
INFLIBNET	Information Library Network	1992
JANET	Joint Academic Network	1984
MALIBNET	Madras Library Network	1992
MYLIBNET	Mysore Library Network	1994
NICNET	National Informatic Centre Network	1977
OCLC	Online Computer Library Centre	1967
RLIN	Research Libraries Information Network	1978
WLN	Western Library Network	1972

29. Online Databases

Offline	Online
MEDLARS (1964)	MEDLINE
Chemical abstract (1907)	CA SEARCH
Psychological Abstract (1927)	PSYCH INFO
Biological Abstract (1926)	BIOSIS
Bibliography of Agriculture	AGRICOLA
LISA (1969)	

30. MARC

MARC	Country
USMARC	America
UKMARC	Britain
CANMARC	Canada
AUSMARC	Australia
MABI	Germany
ANNAMARC	Italy
DANMARC	Danish
IBERMARC	Spain
SWEMARC	Sweden

31. Library Software

Name	Developers
Aquas	Ober Information systems, Calcutta
Archives	Minifax electronics systems, Bombay
Book Magic	Meshil Logic, Calicut-Kerala

CAIRS	Leatherhead Research Association-UK
CDS/ISIS (1985)	UNESCO
CDS/ISIS CD ROM version (1989)	UNESCO
CDS/ISIS Windows version (1997)	UNESCO
Delwindows	DELNET
Dspace (2002)	Massachusetts Institute of Technology
Golden Libra	INSDOC, New Delhi
Greenstone (1997)	New Zealand digital library project
Integrated Library	Pragati computers, Pvt Ltd Madras
Koha (1999)	Katipo Communications, New Zealand
Libman	Datapro consultancy, Pune
Libra ITV	Systems, New Delhi
Librarian	Soft aid, Pune
Library Management	Datamatic consultants Pvt Ltd, Mumbai
Library Management Systems U&I	Software Pvt Ltd, Bangalore
Library Manager Systems	Data control Pvt Ltd, Mumbai
Libsoft	ET & T Corporation, New Delhi

Libsys	Libsys Corporation, New Delhi
Maitreyee	CALIBNET
Sanjay (based on CDS/ISIS)	DESIDOC Software Developers
STAIRS	IBM
Wilisys	Wipro, Bangalore

32. Sources of documents-Types

Primary

1. Periodicals
2. Research report
3. Technical report
4. Conference proceedings
5. Official publications
6. Patents
7. Standards
8. Trade literature
9. Thesis & dissertations
10. Laboratory notebooks
11. Diaries & Memoranda
12. Personal files
13. Manuals

Secondary

1. Bibliography
2. Indexing & abstracting service
3. Reviews & state of art literature
4. Monographs

5. Reference books
6. Text books

Tertiary

1. Yearbooks
2. Directories
3. Bibliography of bibliography
4. List of research in progress
5. Guide to information source
6. Progress and Advances

33. Public library acts in Indian states

SL No.	Year	State
1	1948	TamilNadu
2	1960	Andhra Pradesh
3	1965	Karnataka
4	1967	Maharastra
5	1979	West Bengal
6	1988	Manipur
7	1989	Kerala
8	1989	Hariyana
9	1993	Mizoram
10	1994	Goa
11	2002	Gujarat
12	2001	Orissa
13	2005	Uttaranchal
14	2006	UP
15	2006	Rajasthan
16	2007	Chattisgarh
17	2008	Bihar
18	2009	Arunachal Pradesh

34. Library Associations

1. American Library Association (ALA)

Year of establishment : 1876

Head quarters : Chicago

Address : East Haron Street, Chicago, USA

2. Library Association (LA)

Year of establishment : 1877

Head quarters : London

Address : Ring Mount Street, London, UK

3. International Federation of Information & Documentation (FID)

Year of establishment : 1895

Head quarters : Belgium

4. Association for Information Management (ASLIB)

Year of establishment : 1926

Head quarters : London

Address : Old Street, London, UK

Old name : Association for Special Libraries (till 1983).

5. International Federation of Library Associations & Institutions (IFLA)

Year of establishment : 1929

Head quarters : Hague

6. Indian Library Association (ILA)

Year of establishment : 1933

Head quarters : New Delhi (Calcutta was the first Head quarters)

First life member : S.R Ranganathan

Address : Ansal Building, Mukherjee Nagar, Delhi.

7. Indian Association for Special Libraries & Information Centres (IASLIC)

Year of establishment : 1933

Head quarters : Calcutta

Year of establishment : 1955

Address : F29, GTT, Karkukachi, Calcutta..

35. Species of Classification & Classification Schemes

Species of Classification

1. Enumerative scheme of Classification.

   Examples: Library of Congress Classification scheme

   Rider's International Classification

2. Almost Enumerative scheme of Classification.

   Eg: Subject Classification

   Dewey decimal classification

3. Almost Faceted Classification.

   Eg: Universal Decimal Classification

   Bibliographic Classification.

4. Rigidly Faceted Classification.

   Eg: Colon Classification first 3 editions

5. Almost Freely Faceted Classification.

   Eg: Colon Classification first 4, 5 & 6 editions

6. Fully Freely Faceted Classification.

   Eg: Colon Classification first 7th editions

36. Classification Schemes

1. Dewey Decimal Classification (DDC)

Developed by	:	Melville Dewey
Developed in	:	1876
Latest edition	:	23rd was published by OCLC in 2011
Organization	:	10 Main Class, 100 Divisions and 1000 Sections.
Main Classes	:	000- computer sciences, Information & General works 100- Philosophy & Psychology 200- Religion 300- Social science 400-Language 500- Science 600- Technology & Applied sciences 700- Arts 800- Literature 900- History, Geography & Biography
No. of Volumes	:	4
No. of Tables	:	6 (up to 22nd edition, there were 7 tables)
Tables	:	Table-1 Standard Subdivisions Table-2 Geographic areas, Historic Periods, Persons. Table-3 Subdivisions for Art & Literature Table-4 Subdivisions of Individual Languages

Table-5 Ethnic and National groups

Table-6 Languages.

2. Universal Decimal Classification (UDC)

Developed by	:	Paul Autlet & Henry La Fontain
Developed in	:	1904 in French language (based on DDC)
Publishers	:	Up to 1992 FID was the publishers 1992 Onwards UDC Consortium
Notation	:	Mixed notation
Tables	:	2 Kinds-1.Main Tables (Schedule) 2. Auxiliary Table (Common – auxiliary)
Main Table	:	0- Generalities 1- Philosophy & Psychology 2- Religion & Theology 3- Social Sciences 4- ———(vacant) 5- Mathematics & Natural Science 6- Applied Science 7- Arts 8- Language & Literature 9- Geography & History.

3. Library of Congress Classification (LCC)

Developed by	:	Herbert Putnam
Developed in	:	1897 (for classification of LC)

Organization	:	21 Main Classes (each identifies by a single letter)
Main Classes	:	A- General works
		B- Philosophy, Psychology & Religion
		C- Auxiliary science of history
		D- History general & Old world
		E- America History
		F- America Local history
		G- Geography, anthropology & Recreation
		H- Social Sciences
		J- Political Science
		K- Law
		L- Education
		M- Music
		N- Fine arts
		P- Language & Literature
		Q- Science
		R- Medicine
		S- Agriculture
		T- Technology
		U- Military Science
		V- Navel Science
		Z- Bibliography, Library science

4. Colon Classification (CC)

Developed by	:	S.R Ranganathan
Developed in	:	1933
Notation system	:	Mixed notation

Latest edition : 7th (1987)

Base : 5 Fundamental Categories

P- Personality (,)

M-Matter (;)

E- Energy (:)

S- Space (.)

T- Time (‘)

Main Class : a- Generalia & Bibliography

2- Library Science

A- Sciences

B- Mathematics

C- Physics

D- Engineering

E- Chemistry

F- Technology

G- Biology

H- Geology

HZ- Mining

I- Botany

J- Agriculture

K- Zoology

KZ- Animal Husbandry

L- Medicine

LZ- Pharmacognosy

M- Use full Arts

“- Mysticm & spiritual exp.

N- Fine arts

O- Literature

P- Linguistics

Q- Religion
R- Philosophy
S- Psychology
T- Education
U- Geography
V- History
W- Political science
X- Economics
Y- Sociology
Z- Law

37. National Bibliographies

BNB- (British National Bibliography)

Year of establishment	:	1950
Periodicity	:	Weekly
Parts	:	Alphabetical and classified
	:	Monthly, quarterly, half yearly and annual cumulations are Available for alphabetical part; and classified part is cumulated once in five year.
Classification scheme used	:	DDC
Indexing technique	:	COPASS (Since 1991) PRECIS (1974-1991), (up to 1974 Chain indexing was used)

INB- (Indian National Bibliography)

Year of establishment : 1957

Periodicity : Monthly

Parts : Alphabetical and classified

Classification scheme used : DDC

Coverage : the following publications are excluded-maps, musical Scores, periodicals(except first issue), guide to textbook, Ephemeral and such other materials.

38. Major Journals in Library Science

1. DESIDEOC Journal of Library and Information Technology

   Periodicity : Quarterly

   Publishers : DESIDOC – New Delhi

   Address : DESIDOC
   Ministry of Defence, Metcalfe House, New Delhi- 110 054.

2. Library Progress (International)

   Periodicity : Half Yearly

   Publishers : Dr. A.K Sharma
   Editor in chief

   Address : 115 RPS-DDA Flat, Mansarovar Park, Shahadara, Delhi- 110 032 India.

3. IUP Journal of Knowledge Management

   Periodicity : Quarterly

   Publishers : IUP Publications

Address : Srinagar Colony
Hyderabad, Andhra Pradesh.
www.iupindi.in

4. IASLIC Bulletin

Periodicity : Quarterly
Publishers : IASLIC- Kolkatta
Address : P 291,CIT Scheme No.6M Kangurkachi, Kolkatta.
www.iaslic1955.org.in

5. SRELS Journal of Information Management

Periodicity : Quarterly
Publishers : Sarada Ranganathan Endowment for Library science
Address : 702, Upstairs, 42nd Cross, IIIrd Block, Rajaji Nagar, Bangalore.-560 010.

6. Information Studies

Periodicity : Quarterly
Publishers : Business Manager, Information Studies
Address : 702, Upstairs, 42nd Cross, IIIrd Block, Rajaji Nagar, Bangalore.-560 010.

7. IFLA Journal

Periodicity : Quarterly
Publishers : IFLA
Address : www.sagepublications.com

8. Annals of Library and Information Studies

Periodicity : Quarterly
Publishers : NISCAIR-New Delhi
Address : NISCAIE- New Delhi- 110 012

9. Journal of Library and Information Technology
   Periodicity : Half Yearly
   Publishers : The Library Publications
   Address : The Library Publications 11-A , Adesh Nagar, Kendriya Hindi Sanstan Marg, Agra (UP).
10. ILA Bulletin
   Periodicity : Quarterly
   Publishers : ILA- New Delhi
   Address : Indian Library Association A/40-41, Flat No. 201, Ansal Bulding, Dr.Mukherjee Nagar, New Delhi- 110 009.
11. Library Herald
   Periodicity : Quarterly
   Publishers : Delhi Library Association
   Address : Ranganathan Bhavan C-Block, Community Centre, Naraina Vihar, New Delhi- 110 028.
12. Kelpro Bulletin
   Periodicity : Bi-Annual
   Publishers : Kerala Library Professional Organisation
   Address : Po. Box No. 5543 Kerala University (PO), Thiruvananthapuram- 695 034, Kerala.
13. Pearl- Journal of Library and Information Science
   Periodicity : Quarterly
   Publishers : University Library Teacher's Association of A.P
   Address : B-9, A- Block, L.S.C, Naraina Vihar, New Delhi- 110 028.

39. Greatest Personalities

Antonny Panizzi

Born in 1797 in Italy

Died in 1879

Started his career as a lawyer

Moved to England in 1823 and became the librarian

Developed *British Museum Code* in 1841

Bill Gates

Full Name: William Henry Bill Gates

Born in 1955 in America

Career: Owner and Chairman of Microsoft

In 1973 He became a student of Harvard University

Micro soft Windows was developed by Microsoft in 1983.

C.A Cutter

Full Name : Charles Ammi Cutter

Born in 1837 in America

Died in 1903

Developed *Expansive Classification Scheme* in 1891

Book: *Rules for Dictionary Catalogue* (1876)

Charles Babbage

Born in 1791 in England

Died in 1871

Known as father of Computer

Developed *Analytical Engine.*

E.C Richardson

Born in 1860 in America

Died in 1939

Regarded as the first Classificationist.

Book: *Classification; theoretical and practical*

E.E Hulme

Born in 1859 in England

Died in 1954

Developed the "*theory of literary warrant*"

Career: librarian of Patent office library- London.

Eugene Garfield

Born in 1925 in New York

Founded Institute of Scientific Information in 1955

Developed – *Current Content and Science Citation Index.*

F.W Lancaster

Full Name: Frederick Wilfred Lancaster

Born in 1933 in America

Coined the term *"Paperless society"*

F.W Taylor

Full name: Frederick Winslow Taylor

Born in 1856 in America

Died in1915

Known as *Father of Scientific Management*

George Boole

Born in 1815 at Lincolnshire –England

Died 1864 at Ireland

Developer of Boolean Logic (AND, OR, NOT) in 1847

Career: Mathematics Professor in Queens College.

H.E Bliss

Full Name: He Eyelyn Bliss

Born in 1870 in New York ,America

Died in 1955

He is the developer of *Bibliographic classification scheme* in 1935

Books: *Organisation of Knowledge and systems of science*

Organisation of Knowledge in libraries and subject approach to books.

H.P Luhn

Full name: Hans Peter Luhn

Born in 1896 in Germany

Career: computer scientist for IBM

Developed *Automatic Indexing* in 1950

J.D Brown

Born in 1862 in England

Died in: 1914

Career: Librarian

He developed the "*General theory of Library Classification*".

Developed new classification scheme- *Subject Classification* in 1906

Melville Dewey

Known as father of Modern Librarianship

Full Name: Melville Louise Kossuth Dewey

Date of Birth :10/12/1851 at Adams City

Date of Death: 26/12/1931

1883 –Dewey became Librarian of Columbia College (Now Columbia University)

1876 He founded ALA

1887 He founded First library school in the world.

S.R Ranganathan

Known as Father of Indian Library Science

Mourise Goyer called Ranganathan as Father of Indian Library science.

Full Name: Shiali Ramamrit Ranganathan Ayyer

Date of Birth	:	12/08/1892 at Madras
Date of Death	:	27/09/1972 at Mysore
Father	:	Ramamrit Ayyer
Wife	:	Sarada

PG in Mathematics

BHU (Banaras Hindu University) gave D.Lit

1924	He went to England
1931	Five Laws of Library science was published
1933	First Edition of Colon Classification came out.
1933	Enrolled himself as the first life member of ILA
1937	Prolegomena to library classification
1938	Theory of library catalogue
1945	Elements of library classification
1948	Classification and international documentation

1945-54 Served as Librarian & Professor in BHU

1962	Founded DRTC and became Head
1965	Govt. of India honored wit title of National Research Professor in Library science
1967	Published Prolegomena to library classification

Tim Berners Lee

Born in 1955 in England

Developed World Wide Web (WWW) in 1990

Director of World Wide Web Consortium founded in 1994

Book: *Weaving the* web.

Vint Cerf

Born in 1943 in America

Known as father of internet

Developed ARPANET in 1969.

W.C.B Sayers

Full Name: William Charles Berwick Sayers

Born in 1881in England

Died in 1960

Popularly known as *Grammarian of library classification*

He was the teacher of S.R Ranganathan at London.

Books: *Canon of Classification*

Grammar of Classification

Part-2 :
General Questions
(Subject Wise)

1. Foundations of Library & Information Science
2. Library & Information Centre Management
3. Knowledge Organisation- Classification
4. Knowledge Organisation- Cataloguing
5. Information Science
6. Information Technology

1. Foundations of Library & Information Science

1. How many Library Science Laws are there, according to Ranganathan?

   (a) 3 (b) 4

   (c) 5 (d) 6

2. Five Laws of Library Science was first published in-

   (a) 1928 (b) 1931

   (c) 1933 (d) 1935

3. Which of the Five Laws emphasizes the obligation of the state to enact library legislation?

   (a) First Law (b) Second Law

   (c) Third Law (d) Fourth Law

4. Which of the following law indicates that documents of the library should be brought to the notice of the users?

   (a) First Law (b) Second Law

   (c) Third Law (d) Fourth Law

5. Extension service to blind is justified by which law?

   (a) First Law (b) Second Law

   (c) Third Law (d) Fourth Law

6. Which law necessitates the use of information technology in Libraries?

   (a) Second Law (b) Third Law

   (c) Fourth Law (d) Fifth Law

Answer : 1. (c) 2. (b) 3. (b) 4. (c) 5. (b) 6. (c)

7. Which law implies weeding out of books from library?
   (a) Second Law (b) Third Law
   (c) Fourth Law (d) Fifth Law
8. Which law of library science is related with growth of library?
   (a) Second Law (b) Third Law
   (c) Fourth Law (d) Fifth Law
9. In which law of library science, concept of 'child growth and Adult growth' has been discussed?
   (a) Second Law (b) Third Law
   (c) Fourth Law (d) Fifth Law
10. Location of library building is an implication of which law of library science?
   (a) First Law (b) Second Law
   (c) Third Law (d) Fourth Law
11. The five Laws of Library science is an example of which kind of research?
   (a) Applied research
   (b) Fundamental research
   (c) Pure research
   (d) Survey research
12. A variant to the second law of library science is -
   (a) Closed access
   (b) Open access
   (c) Books for limited users
   (d) Books for all

Answer : 7. (d) 8. (d) 9. (d) 10. (a) 11. (b) 12. (d)

13. Academic libraries are—
    (a) Libraries related with schools
    (b) Libraries related with colleges
    (c) Libraries related with universities
    (d) Libraries related with academic institutions
14. Those who, comes to make use of libraries are called
    (a) Readers (b) Members
    (c) Users (d) Customers
15. The users of libraries in America are called
    (a) Readers (b) Members
    (c) Clients (d) Patrons
16. Public law 480 (pl48) is a/an —— law
    (a) Indian (b) British
    (c) Canadian (d) American
17. How many Indian states have passed library legislation so far?
    (a) 15 (b) 17
    (c) 18 (d) 20
18. Which of the Indian state passed library legislation first?
    (a) Kerala (b) Tamilnadu
    (c) Karnataka (d) Maharastra
19. Library Act in Tamilnadu is popularly known as –
    (a) Madras library Act
    (b) Chennai library Act
    (c) Connimara library Act
    (d) Tamilnadu library Act

Answer : 13. (d) 14. (c) 15. (d) 16. (d) 17. (c) 18. (b) 19. (a)

20. Which of the Indian state recently passed library legislation?

(a) Rajasthan (b) Chattisgarh

(c) Jammu & Kashmir (d) Arunachal Pradesh

21. Author's right to claim ownership of a created work is known as –

(a) Copyright (b) Patent

(c) Monopoly (d) Ownership

22. P.V Varghese prize is awarded by ILA for –

(a) Best library

(b) Best librarian

(c) Best library science teacher

(d) Best article

23. Public library development in India as a movement was initially started from

(a) New Delhi (b) Madras

(c) Baroda (d) Bangalore

24. Which was the first commission appointed by the British Government for the development of libraries in India?

(a) Hunter Commission

(b) Sadler Commission

(c) Mudaliyar Commission

(d) Kothari Commission

25. Who was the first chairman of UGC?

(a) Kothari (b) C.D Deshmugh

(c) S. Radhakrishnan (d) S.R Ranganathan

Answer : 20. (d) 21. (d) 22. (d) 23. (c) 24. (a) 25. (b)

26. UGC is a ——— organization
    (a) Government (b) Semi- Government
    (c) Private (d) Autonomous
27. Which was the first commission in Independent India appointed for the development of education and libraries?
    (a) Radhakrishna Commission
    (b) Ranganathan commission
    (c) Knowledge commission
    (d) Kothari commission
28. Mudaliyar commission was specially set up to
    (a) Primary education
    (b) Secondary education
    (c) Higher secondary education
    (d) Technical education
29. Chief Officer of National Library is known as
    (a) Librarian (b) Manager
    (c) Director (d) Library officer
30. Who established Delhi public library in 1950?
    (a) Government of Delhi
    (b) Government of India
    (c) INESCO
    (d) Government of India with UNESCO
31. Which is the largest public library in South East Asia?
    (a) Calcutta public library
    (b) Delhi public library
    (c) Asiatic society of India
    (d) Connymara pubic library

Answer : 26. (d) 27. (a) 28. (b) 29. (c) 30. (d) 31. (b)

32. Who was associated with imperial library act in 1902?

(a) Lord Curzon (b) Lord Willington

(c) Lord Irvin (d) Lord Minto

33. National library of India is located at

(a) Chennai (b) Bangalore

(c) Kolkatta (d) New Delhi

34. What was the name of librarian who was invited by Punjab University?

(a) A.Panizzi (b) W.Borden

(c) C.A Cutter (d) A. Dickinson

35. Dickinson was hailing from which country?

(a) America (b) Britain

(c) France (d) Italy

36. In which year Dickinson came India?

(a) 1910 (b) 1912

(c) 1915 (d) 1917

37. Shiyaji Gaykwad brought by whom for improvement of library service in Baroda

(a) Dewey (b) Dickinson

(c) Fosket (d) W.Borden

38. W.Borden was belonged to which country?

(a) France (b) Canada

(c) America (d) Britain

39. In which year Borden came to India?

(a) 1910 (b) 1911

(c) 1912 (d) 1915

Answer : 32. (a) 33. (c) 34. (d) 35. (a) 36. (c) 37. (d) 38. (c) 39. (b)

40. Under the 'Delivery of books act' how many copies of books are to be sent to National Library of India?

    (a) 2 (b) 3

    (c) 4 (d) 5

41. The headquarters of American Library Association is at

    (a) Hague (b) Chicago

    (c) New York (d) California

42. Librarian of Library of Congress is appointed by

    (a) US President

    (b) President of LC

    (c) US Parliament

    (d) Chairman, Parliamentary council

43. Which of the following states levies library cess on either property tax or house tax?

    (a) West Bengal (b) Kerala

    (c) Hariyana (d) Karnataka

44. School of librarianship is located at-

    (a) New Delhi (b) New York

    (c) London (d) Chicago

45. Who opened the first "School of library economy "

    (a) Bordon (b) Dickinson

    (c) Ranganathan (d) Dewey

46. The head quarters of Commonwealth Library Association is at

    (a) Nigeria (b) New Delhi

    (c) Colombo (d) Islamabad

Answer : 40. (c) 41. (b) 42. (a) 43. (c) 44. (c) 45. (d) 46. (a)

47. 'Book week' in India is celebrated every year in which month?
    (a) January (b) November
    (c) September (d) December
48. The *advisory committee for libraries* appointed by Govt. of India is also known as-
    (a) Sinha Committee
    (b) Kothari Commission
    (c) Ranganathan Committee
    (d) Library Committee
49. Radhakrishna Commission is also known as
    (a) Secondary Education Commission
    (b) University Education Commission
    (c) Kothari Commission
    (d) Sinha Committee
50. Mudaliyar Commission is also known as
    (a) Library Committee
    (b) Kothari Commission
    (c) Secondary Education Commission
    (d) Ranganathan Committee
51. In India, working group on libraries was set up by
    (a) Human Resource Department
    (b) Planning Commission
    (c) Information Technology Department
    (d) Social & Cultural Department
52. Who was the first librarian of National Library Calcutta?
    (a) S.R Ranganathan (b) Asadulla
    (c) S.K Pandey (d) B.S Kesavan

Answer : 47. (b) 48. (a) 49. (b) 50. (c) 51. (b) 52. (d)

53. Head quarters of Raja Ram Mohan Roy Library Foundation is located at
    (a) Calcutta (b) New Delhi
    (c) Mumbai (d) Madras
54. Raja Ram Mohan Roy Library Foundation is mainly concentrated with the promotion of what kind of libraries?
    (a) Academic Libraries (b) Public Libraries
    (c) University Libraries (d) Special Libraries
55. Connemara public library is situated at
    (a) Kolkatta (b) New Delhi
    (c) Chennai (d) Bangalore
56. Khuda Baksh oriental public library is located at
    (a) Simla (b) Patna
    (c) Secunderabad (d) Hyderabad
57. Asiatic society library is situated at
    (a) Mumbai (b) Patna
    (c) Ghaziabad (d) Mysore
58. Ranganathan was appointed as National research professor in Library Science by Govt. of India in
    (a) 1960 (b) 1965
    (c) 1968 (d) 1970
59. The Concept of *librametry* was developed by
    (a) E.L Foskett (b) J.H Shera
    (c) S.R Ranganathan (d) Paul Autlet
60. Who coined the term *paperless society?*
    (a) S.R Ranganathan (b) F.W Lancaster
    (c) F.W Taylor (d) Calvin Moores

Answer : 53. (a) 54. (b) 55. (c) 56. (b) 57. (a) 58. (b) 59. (c) 60. (b)

61. Library of Congress is located at
    (a) New York (b) Chicago
    (c) California (d) Washington DC
62. Library of Congress is established in the year
    (a) 1750 (b) 1789
    (c) 1800 (d) 1902
63. Saraswadi Mahal Manuscript library is located at
    (a) Madras (b) Tanjaore
    (c) Coimbatore (d) Tiruchirappally
64. National library for blind and physically handicapped is located at
    (a) Dehradoon (b) Patna
    (c) Delhi (d) Hyderabad
65. What is the name of library of UNO?
    (a) Library of Edison
    (b) Abraham Linkon library
    (c) Dag Hamerscold library
    (d) New York International Library
66. Name the college in which Dewey worked as student library assistant.
    (a) Montieth college (b) Amherst college
    (c) Ohio college (d) Adams college
67. How many digits are there in ISBN?
    (a) 8 (b) 10
    (c) 12 (d) 13
68. When was ISBN started in the world?
    (a) 1970 (b) 1972
    (c) 1985 (d) 1995

Answer : 61. (d) 62. (c) 63. (b) 64. (a) 65. (c)
66. (b) 67. (d) 68. (b)

69. When was ISBN started in India?
   (a) 1972 (b) 1975
   (c) 1982 (d) 1985
70. How many blocks are there in ISBN?
   (a) 3 (b) 4
   (c) 5 (d) 6
71. How many digits are there in ISSN?
   (a) 8 (b) 10
   (c) 12 (d) 13
72. How many blocks are there in ISSN?
   (a) 2 (b) 3
   (c) 4 (d) 5
73. Which is the national agency in India to provide ISBN?
   (a) ILA
   (b) Raja Ram Mohan Roy National Agency
   (c) Delhi Public library
   (d) DRTC
74. In which date ISBN became in the present form (13 digit form)?
   (a) Jan1 2005 (b) Jan1 2006
   (c) Jan1 2007 (d) Jan1 2008
75. ISBN was developed by whom?
   (a) Gorden Foster (b) Philip Kotler
   (c) E.L Foskette (d) S.R Ranganathan
76. Right to education Act was passed by Govt. of Indian in which year?
   (a) 2005 (b) 2008
   (c) 2009 (d) 2010

Answer : 69. (d) 70. (c) 71. (a) 72. (a) 73. (b) (c). 75. (a) 76. (c)

77. Right to education Act ensures
    (a) Free education for children
    (b) Compulsory education for children
    (c) Free and compulsory education for children
    (d) Free education with food
78. Kesavan Institute of Information and Knowledge management is located at
    (a) Bangalore (b) Mysore
    (c) Hyderabad (d) Delhi

Answer : 77. (c) 78. (b)

2. Library & Information Centre Management

1. What are the three levels of management?
   (a) Primary, Secondary, Tertiary
   (b) First, Second, Third
   (c) Top, Middle, Operational
   (d) None of these
2. Who is the father of Scientific Management?
   (a) F.W Tailor (b) Gullic
   (c) Hentry Fayol (d) Abraham Maslow
3. Who is considered as 'father of Human relation movement'?
   (a) Elton Mayo (b) F.W Taylor
   (c) Hentry Fayol (d) Gullic
4. Who Father of Classical school of management?
   (a) Gullic (b) Hentry Fayol
   (c) F.W Tailor (d) Peter Druker
5. Who Introduced *Need theory*?
   (a) Peter Druker (b) Abraham Maslow
   (c) F.W Tailor (d) Hentry Fayol
6. Who among the following is related with 'theory of X and theory of Y'
   (a) Abraham Maslow (b) F.W Tailor
   (c) Hentry Fayol (d) Douglas Mc Gregore
7. Acronym of POSDCORB is coined by
   (a) F.W Tailor
   (b) Abraham Maslow
   (c) L Gullic and L Urwick
   (d) Hentry Fayol

Answer : 1. (c) 2. (a) 3. (a) 4. (b) 5. (b) 6. (d) 7. (c)

8. Who among the following is related with *General system theory?*
   (a) Ludwing V Bertlanfly (b) L Gullic and L Urwick
   (c) Hentry Fayol (d) F.W Tailor
9. Who among the following is related with *Management by objectives?*
   (a) Hentry Fayol (b) Peter Drucker
   (c) F.W Tailor (d) Abraham Maslow
10. Fourteen Principles of management is coined by
    (a) Hentry Fayol (b) S.R Ranganathan
    (c) F.W Tailor (d) Douglas Mc Greogore
11. *Operations research* is a tool of
    (a) Library management (b) Library cataloguing
    (c) Library classification (d) Reference service
12. MBO concept came into existence in
    (a) 1940s (b) 1950s
    (c) 1960s (d) 1970s
13. The basic theory regarding human motivation is propounded by
    (a) Maslow (b) Mayo
    (c) Taylor (d) Fayol
14. Hentry Fayol belongs to
    (a) Classical school
    (b) Human relation school
    (c) Decision making school
    (d) None of these
15. Espirit De Corps means
    (a) Doing nothing (b) Doing something
    (c) Team work (d) Team spirit

Answer : 8. (a) 9. (b) 10. (a) 11. (a) 12. (b)
13. (a) 14. (a) 15. (c)

16. The scalar chain in management is
    (a) Structure authority
    (b) Scale of pay
    (c) Total number of staffs
    (d) Chain links
17. The process of analysis of job into different distinct items are called
    (a) Job analysis (b) Job study
    (c) Work analysis (d) Work study
18. The meaning of cost benefit analysis is
    (a) Evaluation based on cost
    (b) Evaluation based on benefit
    (c) Evaluation based on benefit in relation to cost
    (d) Evaluation based on money
19. PERT means
    (a) Technique for job description
    (b) Technique for system analysis
    (c) Technique for job analysis
    (d) Technique for data collection
20. The study of relation between work and time by using chart is called
    (a) System approach (b) System analysis
    (c) Job analysis (d) Job Study
21. Who coined the term 'initiation of readers' first
    (a) Dewey (b) Ranganathan
    (c) Bliss (d) Cutter
22. Systematic use of user's education is the contribution of –
    (a) Ptrip B Knap (b) Melvil Dewey
    (c) Ranganathan (d) E.L Coates

Answer : 16. (a) 17. (a) 18. (c) 19. (c) 20. (a) 21. (b) 22. (a)

23. Which institution experimented user's education for the first time?
    (a) Delhi university library
    (b) Montieth College
    (c) Ohio College
    (d) London school of arts
24. Odd one out
    (a) Bibliography (b) Publishers catalogue
    (c) Accession register (d) Book sellers catalogue
25. Drury's principle is related with
    (a) Book selection (b) Classification
    (c) Cataloguing (d) Library management
26. McClovin's principle is related with
    (a) Book selection (b) Classification
    (c) Cataloguing (d) Library management
27. The book selection principle 'Right book to right readers at the right time' is developed by
    (a) Dewey (b) McClovin
    (c) Ranganathan (d) Drury
28. Demand theory of book selection is developed by
    (a) Dewey (b) McClovin
    (c) Ranganathan (d) Drury
29. 'To provide best book to the maximum readers at the least cost' is the book selection principle of –
    (a) Dewy (b) McClovin
    (c) Ranganathan (d) Drury
30. What is budget?
    (a) Annual estimate of income
    (b) Annual estimate of expenditure
    (c) Annual estimate of income and expenditure
    (d) Comparison of income and expenditure

Answer : 23. (b) 24. (c) 25. (a) 26. (a) 27. (d) 28. (b) 29. (a) 30. (c)

31. What percentage of the total money should be spent on binding of according to Ranganathan?
    (a) 20 (b) 25
    (c) 5 (d) 10
32. On which item the most of the money of the budget of library is spent
    (a) Books (b) Periodicals
    (c) Staffs (d) Binding
33. According to UGC, what percentage of total money to be spent on the salaries of the staffs
    (a) 25 (b) 40
    (c) 50 (d) 60
34. Who approves the budget of the college library?
    (a) Library Committee (b) Principal
    (c) UGC (d) State Govt.
35. Funds of special libraries are provided by
    (a) Parental organization (b) UGC
    (c) Library cess (d) Central Govt.
36. For a University library, what should be the percentage of the total budget according to UGC?
    (a) 5 (b) 6.5
    (c) 8 (d) 10
37. The method of budgeting which is not concerned with past, but concerned with the requirements of the future is called
    (a) Line budgeting
    (b) Programming budgeting
    (c) Formulae budgeting
    (d) Zero- based budgeting

Answer : 31. (c) 32. (c) 33. (c) 34. (b) 35. (a) 36. (b) 37. (d)

38. Most of money of the library budget is spent?
   (a) For books (b) For periodicals
   (c) For staff salary (d) For furniture
39. Scrutiny of financial transaction is known as
   (a) Budgeting (b) Accounting
   (c) Auditing (d) Scrutiny
40. Who introduced Browne charging system?
   (a) Neena E Brown (b) J.D Brown
   (c) S.R Ranganathan (d) Melvil Dewey
41. What is *pamphlet*?
   (a) An unbound book
   (b) A book having less than 49 printed pages
   (c) A book having more than 1000 pages
   (d) A spiritual book
42. The standard size of an *accession register* is
   (a) 15" X 13" (b) 16" X 13"
   (c) 12" X 10" (d) 5" X 8"
43. The standard size of card catalogue is
   (a) 7.5cm X 12.5cm (b) 6.5cm X 10.5cm
   (c) 8cm X 10cm (d) 7.5cm X 15cm
44. Who introduced electrically operated charging system first?
   (a) Neena E Brown (b) S.R Ranganathan
   (c) James Duff Brown (d) Gaylord Brother
45. Who invented 'Color Charging system'?
   (a) Neena E Browne (b) Ranganathan
   (c) Dewey (d) Walter H Kaiser

Answer : 38. (c) 39. (c) 40. (a) 41. (b) 42. (b)
43. (a) 44. (d) 45. (d)

46. Which is the most popular circulation system (conventional) in libraries?
   (a) Newark charging system
   (b) Dummy system
   (c) Register system
   (d) Browne system
47. What is the main record of a library?
   (a) Accession register (b) Catalogue
   (c) Shelf list (d) Issue register
48. The mobile libraries are called as— by Ranganathan
   (a) Bus Library (b) Librachine
   (c) Moving library (d) Mobile library
49. Mobile library is a kind of –
   (a) Inter library loan (b) Cooperative service
   (c) Extension service (d) Resource sharing
50. *Three card system* is used in libraries for
   (a) Circulation of books
   (b) Circulation of periodicals
   (c) Acquisition and control of periodicals
   (d) Reservation of books
51. Who introduced *three card systems*?
   (a) S.R Ranganathan (b) Neena E Brown
   (c) C.ACutter (d) P.N Kaula
52. The term 'bespeaking' means
   (a) Photocopying of books
   (b) Returning of books
   (c) Issuing of books
   (d) Reservation of books

Answer : 46. (d) 47. (a) 48. (b) 49. (c) 50. (c)
51. (a) 52. (d)

53. KARDEX system is used for
    (a) Keeping records of books
    (b) Keeping records of periodicals
    (c) Keeping records of CDs
    (d) Keeping records of bound volumes
54. KARDEX system was devised by
    (a) Madras public library
    (b) Delhi public library
    (c) Library of Congress
    (d) Remington Rand of India.Ltd.
55. 'Book Ends' means
    (a) End page of the book (b) Book support
    (c) Digital library (d) CDs
56. What term is used for blank leaf either starting or end of the book?
    (a) Vacant leaf (b) Free leaf
    (c) Fly leaf (d) Whit leaf
57. Who coined the term 'librametry'?
    (a) Lancaster (b) Alan Pritchard
    (c) Berwick Sayers (d) S.R Ranganathan
58. Into how many classes, users of library can be classified according to Ranganathan?
    (a) 4 (b) 5
    (c) 6 (d) 7
59. Who is a 'bibliopegist'?
    (a) One who prepares bibliography?
    (b) One who binds books?
    (c) One who Xerox books
    (d) One who rectify books

Answer : 53. (b) 54. (d) 55. (b) 56. (c) 57. (d) 58. (c) 59. (b)

60. '*Biblot*' is a technical name of
  (a) Reference book
  (b) Unknown authored book
  (c) Rare book
  (d) Small book
61. What is 'bibliopoly'?
  (a) Xeroxing books
  (b) Binding of books
  (c) Sale of rare books
  (d) Purchasing of rare books
62. As per the norms prescribed by UNESCO, a book should have at least .... Pages
  (a) 45 (b) 49
  (c) 50 (d) 99
63. The direct method of electro stat copying is called
  (a) Reprography (b) Xerography
  (c) Photography (d) Electro fax
64. The Indirect method of electro stat copying is called
  (a) Xerography (b) Reprography
  (c) Photography (d) Electro fax
65. What is '*Aisle?*'
  (a) The passage between two parallel book racks
  (b) The reading space of library
  (c) Refreshment area in the library
  (d) Technical section of the library
66. The Register card, Check card, and classified index card are used in
  (a) Circulation
  (b) Three card system
  (c) Kardex system
  (d) Brwoney charging system

Answer : 60. (d) 61. (c) 62. (b) 63. (d) 64. (a) 65. (a) 66. (b)

67. Shelf list card
    (a) Represent each volume in the shelf
    (b) Replicate the arrangement in the shelf
    (c) Are used for stock verification
    (d) All the above

Answer : 67. (d)

3. Knowledge Organisation-Classification

1. Who gave three steps for classification, i.e. to class, classify and classification.
   (a) Ranganathan (b) Dewey
   (c) Bliss (d) Sayers
2. Division into two is called
   (a) Dichotomy (b) Decachotomy
   (c) Polychotomy (d) Monochotomy
3. Classes belongs to same array are called
   (a) Coordinate class (b) Subordinate class
   (c) Super ordinate class (d) Canonical class
4. What is the indicator digit for space in UDC?
   (a) Hyphen (b) Dot
   (c) Circular bracket (d) Square bracket
5. How many kinds of auxiliaries are recognized in UDC?
   (a) 2 (b) 3
   (c) 4 (d) 5
6. According to Ranganathan, how many mnemonics are there?
   (a) 2 (b) 3
   (c) 4 (d) 5
7. How many steps are there, for classification according to Ranganathan?
   (a) 6 (b) 7
   (c) 8 (d) 9

Answer : 1. (c) 2. (a) 3. (a) 4. (c) 5. (a)
6. (c) 7. (d)

8. Which edition of DDC is known as *standard edition*?
   (a) 15 (b) 18
   (c) 20 (d) 22
9. What is the indicator digit for common isolate in Cutter's expansive classification?
   (a) dot(.) (b) Comma (,)
   (c) Equal to sign (=) (d) Plus sign (+)
10. How many zones have been recognized by Ranganathan for an array?
    (a) 2 (b) 3
    (c) 4 (d) 5
11. Who is a classificationist?
    (a) Those who classify books
    (b) Those who develop classification scheme
    (c) Scholar in classification
    (d) Class1 Officer
12. Who is a classifier?
    (a) One who classify books
    (b) One who develop classification scheme
    (c) Scholar in classification
    (d) Teacher in classification
13. Who devised first bibliographic classification?
    (a) Bacon (b) Dewey
    (c) Genser (d) Bliss
14. Method of residue is to find out the
    (a) Personality facet (b) Matter facet
    (c) Energy facet (d) Space facet

Answer : 8. (a) 9. (a) 10. (d) 11. (b) 12. (a) 13. (d) 14. (a)

15. Who developed the *dynamic theory of library classification?*
    (a) Dewey (b) Ranganathan
    (c) Richardson (d) Bacon
16. What are modes of formation of subjects?
    (a) Generation of new subjects
    (b) Formation of new subjects
    (c) Evolution of subjects
    (d) Origin of new subjects
17. Who gave the term *modes of formation of subjects?*
    (a) Ranganathan (b) Dewey
    (c) Sayers (d) Cutter
18. Pure subjects are obtained by which modes of formation?
    (a) Fission (b) Fusion
    (c) Denudation (d) Distillation
19. Complex subjects are obtained by which modes of formation?
    (a) Fission (b) Fusion
    (c) Loose Assemblage (d) Denudation
20. Basic subjects are obtained by which mode of formation?
    (a) Denudation (b) Fission
    (c) Fusion (d) Distillation
21. Bio-technology is an example of generation of knowledge by
    (a) Denudation (b) Loose assemblage
    (c) Fusion (d) Distillation

Answer : 15. (b) 16. (c) 17. (a) 18. (d) 19. (c) 20. (b) 21. (b)

22. The mode of formation of subject *fission* gives
    (a) Basic subject (b) Complicated subject
    (c) Canonical subject (d) Coordinate subjects
23. The mode of formation of subject 'cluster' was formerly known as
    (a) Fusion (b) Subject bundle
    (c) Loose assemblage (d) Denudation
24. How many planes are there in classifying document?
    (a) 3 (b) 4
    (c) 5 (d) 6
25. What is *notational plane*?
    (a) To give some symbol for identity
    (b) To give serial numbers
    (c) To give class numbers
    (d) None of these
26. Who defined *notation as short hand sign*
    (a) Ranganathan (b) Dewey
    (c) Margaret Mann (d) H.E Bliss
27. What type of notations are used in DDC
    (a) Pure (b) Mixed
    (c) Both (d) None of these
28. What type of notations are used in CC
    (a) Pure (b) Mixed
    (c) Both (d) None of these
29. In which year first edition of DDC was published
    (a) 1875 (b) 1876
    (c) 1877 (d) 1879

Answer : 22. (a) 23. (b) 24. (a) 25. (a) 26. (c)
27. (a) 28. (b) 29. (b)

30. How many editions of DDC have been published so far?
    (a) 20 (b) 21
    (c) 22 (d) 23
31. The index of DDC is called
    (a) Subject index (b) Title index
    (c) DDC index (d) Relative index
32. In which year the 22nd edition of DDC was released
    (a) 2001 (b) 2002
    (c) 2003 (d) 2004
33. How many tables are there in DDC 22nd edition?
    (a) 5 (b) 6
    (c) 7 (d) 8
34. From which edition onwards DDC started to publish in the control of web environment?
    (a) 20 (b) 21
    (c) 22 (d) 23
35. In which classification scheme 'zero' is the only connecting symbol
    (a) DDC (b) UDC
    (c) CC (d) IC
36. P-notes are used in which classification
    (a) DDC (b) UDC
    (c) CC (d) IC
37. Who devised Colon Classification (C(C)?
    (a) Dewey (b) Ranganathan
    (c) Bliss (d) Brown

Answer : 30. (c) 31. (d) 32. (c) 33. (b) 34. (c)
35. (a) 36. (b) 37. (b)

38. CC is known Colon Classification, because
    (a) Colon was the only connecting symbol when it was started
    (b) No any reason
    (c) Colon is used along with all numbers
    (d) Colon is the symbol of personality
39. In which year first edition of CC was published
    (a) 1929 (b) 1931
    (c) 1932 (d) 1933
40. Which is the latest edition of CC?
    (a) 5 (b) 6
    (c) 7 (d) 8
41. In which year 7th edition of CC came out
    (a) 1985 (b) 1987
    (c) 1990 (d) 2003
42. The symbol delta (“) is used in CC to indicate
    (a) Fine arts
    (b) Mystics and spiritual experience
    (c) Useful arts
    (d) Linguistics
43. The ordinal value of delta (“) in CC is
    (a) Between M and N (b) Between N and O
    (c) Between L and M (d) Between K and L
44. How many basic subjects are there according to CC?
    (a) 10 (b) 20
    (c) 25 (d) 32

Answer : 38. (a) 39. (d) 40. (c) 41. (b) 42. (b) 43. (a) 44. (d)

45. English capital letter 'T' denotes which subject according to CC
    (a) History (b) Education
    (c) Medicine (d) Religion
46. Who developed subject classification?
    (a) Sayers (b) Bacon
    (c) J.D Brown (d) Cutter
47. In which year *Subject classification* was devised
    (a) 1895 (b) 1906
    (c) 1933 (d) 1915
48. Who devised *Expansive classification*?
    (a) C.A Cutter (b) J.D Brown
    (c) Sayers (d) Putman
49. In which year *expansive classification* was first published?
    (a) 1876 (b) 1891
    (c) 1895 (d) 905
50. Which organization is corporate author of UDC?
    (a) FID (b) IFLA
    (c) UNESCO (d) LC
51. UDC was first published in
    (a) 1895 (b) 1905
    (c) 1914 (d) 1887
52. Who developed *library of Congress Classification*
    (a) Bacon (b) Sayers
    (c) Herbert Putman (d) Brown

Answer : 45. (b) 46. (c) 47. (b) 48. (a) 49. (b)
50. (a) 51. (b) 52. (c)

53. In which year *library of congress classification* scheme was first published

(a) 1891 (b) 1897

(c) 1905 (d) 1914

54. How many main class are there in library of congress classification

(a) 10 (b) 20

(c) 21 (d) 32

55. Hentry La Fontain and Paul Otlet were associated with

(a) DDC (b) CC

(c) UDC (d) LCC

56. According to library *of congress classification Scheme*, which of the following indicates library science?

(a) 2 (b) 020

(c) T (d) Z

57. Who devised *Bibliographic Classification?*

(a) H.E Bliss (b) S.R Ranganathan

(c) J.D Brown (d) Sayers

58. Who devised *International Classification?*

(a) Cutter (b) Rider

(c) Dewey (d) Sayers

59. In which year *International classification* was published

(a) 1905 (b) 1961

(c) 1965 (d) 1950

Answer : 53. (b) 54. (c) 55. (c) 56. (d) 57. (a) 58. (b) 59. (b)

60. How many varieties of phase relations are recognized in7th edition of CC

    (a) 4 (b) 5

    (c) 6 (d) 7

61. Who is the person, who edited DDC seven times?

    (a) Dewey (b) Sayers

    (c) Rider (d) Evelyn Mary Saymour

62. Which abridged edition of UDC is called *International standard abridged edition?*

    (a) 2nd (b) 3rd

    (c) 4th (d) 5th

63. Mnemonics means

    (a) Something aid to memory

    (b) One type of notation system

    (c) One type of array

    (d) None of these

64. How hospitality in chain can be taken

    (a) Gap device

    (b) Empty digit

    (c) Empty emptying digit

    (d) Super imposition device

65. How hospitality in array can be taken

    (a) Gap device (b) Octive device

    (c) Alphabetical device (d) Empty digit

66. How many fundamental categories are according to Ranganathan?

    (a) 3 (b) 4

    (c) 5 (d) 6

Answer : 60. (c) 61. (d) 62. (a) 63. (a) 64. (d) 65. (c) 66. (c)

67. Which one of the following is the core of a subject?
(a) Personality (b) Matter
(c) Energy (d) Space

68. Which of the following symbol is introduced in 7th edition of CC for phase relation?
(a) " (b) &
(c) + (d) =

69. In CC, common isolate 'm' will be applied
(a) Before space facet (b) After space facet
(c) Before time facet (d) After time facet

70. In CC, in schedule of library science (2), Matter facet (M) has been taken from
(a) Not from anywhere
(b) Biography
(c) Generalia bibliography
(d) Computer science

71. In CC, personality facet of History (v) is taken from
(a) Common isolate (b) Language isolate
(c) Time isolate (d) Space isolate

72. The correct sequential order of five fundamental categories
(a) [P][M][E][S][T] (b) [M] [P][[E][S][T]
(c) [T][S][S][E][M][P] (d) [E][P][M}[S][T]

73. Subject arrangement of document is also called
(a) Filiatery sequence (b) Facet sequence
(c) Helpful sequence (d) Facet formula

74. In CC, P2 represents
(a) Second round personality
(b) Second level personality
(c) Second round property
(d) Second level property

Answer : 67. (a) 68. (b) 69. (a) 70. (c) 71. (d)
72. (a) 73. (a) 74. (b)

75. In CC, 2P represents
    (a) Second round personality
    (b) Second level personality
    (c) Second round property
    (d) Second level property
76. The country in which library is located and where classification work is being done, is called
    (a) National country (b) Father country
    (c) Mother country (d) Foreign country
77. How many pages were there, for the first edition of DDC?
    (a) 42 (b) 50
    (c) 101 (d) 142
78. How many steps are there for classifying a document according to Ranganathan?
    (a) 4 (b) 5
    (c) 8 (d) 9
79. Who enunciated five fundamental categories?
    (a) Ranganathan (b) Dewey
    (c) Sayers (d) Brown
80. Who enunciated *Subject classification?*
    (a) Ranganathan (b) Brown
    (c) Sayers (d) Cutter
81. Which of the following is the most popular classification scheme in international level?
    (a) UDC (b) LCC
    (c) DDC (d) CC
82. In CC digit '2' in space isolate stands for
    (a) world (b) Mother country
    (c) India (d) Favored country

Answer : 75. (a) 76. (c) 77. (a) 78. (d) 79. (a) 80. (b) 81. (c) 82. (b)

83. DDC was made available in machine readable form
    (a) 1984 (b) 1985
    (c) 1998 (d) 2003
84. Who conducted DDC online project in 1985?
    (a) LC (b) Forest Press
    (c) Britannica, Inc (d) Europa
85. Which are the three emptying digits postulated in 7th edition of CC?
    (a) XYZ (b) TVU
    (c) TVX (d) VXZ
86. In which classification scheme, *floating tables* are used?
    (a) DDC (b) CC
    (c) LC (d) UDC
87. In classification, the groups – infants, children, adolescents, adults represents
    (a) An array (b) A facet
    (c) A chain (d) A characteristics
88. In CC, parenthesis ( ) is used to indicate
    (a) Geographic device (b) Chronologic device
    (c) Subject device (d) Classic device
89. The term 'Subject Reference Code ' is related to
    (a) Library of Congress Classification
    (b) Universal Decimal Classification
    (c) Broad System of Ordering
    (d) Bibliographic Classification
90. Phoenix schedule is a part of
    (a) DDC (b) UDC
    (c) CC (d) LC

Answer : 83. (a) 84. (b) 85. (c) 86. (c) 87. (a) 88. (c) 89. (c) 90. (a)

91. Phoenix schedule represents
    (a) Classes which are slightly modified
    (b) Classes which are completely changed
    (c) Classes to be modified in future
    (d) Classes not to be modified

92. In which year 23rd edition of DDC came out?
    (a) 2011 (b) 2010
    (c) 2009 (d) 2008

Answer : 91. (b) 92. (a)

4. Knowledge Organisation-Cataloguing

1. Dublin Core is a
   (a) Catalogue code (b) Classification scheme
   (c) Metadata standard (d) Computer programme
2. How many elements are there in Dublin Core?
   (a) 10 (b) 12
   (c) 15 (d) 20
3. Cataloguing in publication was started by
   (a) Indian Library Association
   (b) American Library Association
   (c) British Library
   (d) Library of Congress
4. Cataloguing in publication was started by LC in which year?
   (a) 1969 (b) 1970
   (c) 1971 (d) 1972
5. Searchable term in Chain Index is called –
   (a) Sort link (b) Un sort link
   (c) False link (d) Search link
6. In Chain Indexing Term which is not searched by users is called
   (a) Sort link (b) Un sort link
   (c) False link (d) Un search link
7. In chain Indexing, a word don't contain any word to represent it is called
   (a) Sort link (b) Un sort link
   (c) False link (d) Vacant link

Answer : 1. (c) 2. (c) 3. (d) 4. (c) 5. (a) 6. (b) 7. (c)

8. The entry prepared on words and names that brings variation in the approach to a document is called
   (a) Cross reference Index Entry
   (b) Cross reference Entry
   (c) Book Index Entry
   (d) Class Index Entry
9. The subject analytical entry, prepared for internal part of the document is called
   (a) Cross reference entry
   (b) Cross reference index entry
   (c) Book Index entry
   (d) Class index entry
10. Who said that, *catalogue is a list of books, which is arranged on some definite plan?*
    (a) C.A Cutter (b) W.C.B Sayers
    (c) A. Panizzi (d) Ranganathan
11. Who made the rules of cataloguing first?
    (a) Cutter (b) Panizzi
    (c) Ranganathan (d) Sayers
12. When was 'Cutter's rules for dictionary catalogue 'was first published in
    (a) 1850 (b) 1870
    (c) 1876 (d) 1895
13. The term "pre-natal cataloguing" was coned by?
    (a) Ranganathan (b) Sayers
    (c) Panizzi (d) Cutter
14. Who was the deviser of British *museum code?*
    (a) Panizzi (b) Ranganathan
    (c) Sayers (d) Cutter

Answer : 8. (a) 9. (a) 10. (a) 11. (b) 12. (c) 13. (a) 14. (a)

15. AA Code (Anglo American Code) for cataloguing was published in
    (a) 1876 (b) 1796
    (c) 1908 (d) 1933
16. CCC (Classified Catalogue Code) was published in
    (a) 1931 (b) 1932
    (c) 1933 (d) 1934
17. CCC was developed by
    (a) Sayers (b) Panizzi
    (c) Ranganathan (d) Brown
18. In which year AACR-1 came out?
    (a) 1960 (b) 1967
    (c) 1905 (d) 1978
19. In which year AACR-2 came out?
    (a) 1968 (b) 1970
    (c) 1978 (d) 1989
20. What is the standard size of card catalogue?
    (a) 12.5 X 7.5 mm (b) 12.5 X 7.5 cm
    (c) 15 X 12.5 cm (d) 12.5 X 10.5 cm
21. Pre-natal cataloguing means
    (a) Selective cataloguing
    (b) Descriptive cataloguing
    (c) Cataloguing in source
    (d) Shared cataloguing
22. How many main entries are made for each document?
    (a) 1 (b) 2
    (c) 3 (d) 4

Answer : 15. (c) 16. (d) 17. (c) 18. (b) 19. (c)
20. (b) 21. (c) 22. (a)

23. The name of author of book is not known, it can be called
    (a) Sacred book (b) Pseudonym
    (c) Anonyms (d) Antonyms
24. In chain procedure, connecting symbols signify which type of links ?
    (a) Sort link (b) Un sort link
    (c) False link (d) True link
25. According to AACR-2, the size of the book in physical description area is preceded by
    (a) Colon (b) Semi colon
    (c) Full stop (d) Comma
26. Tracing is in CCC on
    (a) In the bottom of main entry
    (b) In the middle of main entry
    (c) On the back of main entry
    (d) On the right hand side of back of main entry
27. Name of the author assumed by him to conceal his identity is called
    (a) Pseudonym (b) Personal name
    (c) Parallel name (d) Alternative name
28. How the name of the author is shown in the main entry, if the author's name has been taken from outside of the book?
    (a) Italic
    (b) Within inverted commas
    (c) Within square bracket
    (d) Within circular bracket

Answer : 23. (c) 24. (c) 25. (b) 26. (d) 27. (a) 28. (c)

29. If the name of the editor is given on the title page of the book, the main entry will be prepared under which of the following, according to AACR-2 ?
    (a) Editor (b) Author
    (c) Title (d) Collaborator
30. The concept of 'systematic indexing' was devised by
    (a) Faradane (b) Ranganathan
    (c) Coats (d) Luhn
31. KWIC indexing system was developed by
    (a) H.P Luhn (b) Ranganathan
    (c) E.J Coates (d) C.A Cutter
32. UNITERM indexing was developed by
    (a) Ranganathan (b) H.P Luhn
    (c) M. Taub (d) E.J Coates
33. Who developed chain indexing?
    (a) H.P Luhn (b) Ranganathan
    (c) M.Taub (d) Faradane
34. The Controlled vocabulary in indexing means
    (a) Dictionary (b) Thesaurus
    (c) Vocabulary (d) Synonyms
35. Who started science citation index?
    (a) F.W Lancaster (b) Ranganathan
    (c) Eugene Garfield (d) Foskette
36. Who invented dictionary catalogue?
    (a) Ranganathan (b) C.A Cutter
    (c) Lancaster (d) M.Taub
37. What is the thickness of a library catalogue?
    (a) 0.025 mm (b) 0.025 cm
    (c) 0.25mm (d) 0.25cm

Answer : 29. (c) 30. (a) 31. (a) 32. (c) 33. (b) 34. (b) 35. (c) 36. (b) 37. (b)

38. How many parts are there, for each formats of CCF?
    (a) 2 (b) 3
    (c) 4 (d) 5
39. Which of the following is not a quality of a notation?
    (a) Brevity (b) Simplicity
    (c) Flexibility (d) Hospitality
40. See references are shown in Seer's list of subject headings by
    (a) X (b) XY
    (c) XZ (d) None of these
41. Who used the term 'pre-natal cataloguing' for the first time?
    (a) Ranganathan (b) Sayers
    (c) Cutter (d) Faradane
42. What is another name of 'Normative principles 'of cataloguing given by Ranganathan?
    (a) Canon of classification
    (b) Canon of cataloguing
    (c) Canon of Indexing
    (d) Canon of abstracting
43. Library of Congress List of Subject Headings (LCSH) was formulated in
    (a) 1876 (b) 1897
    (c) 1895 (d) 1899
44. Who designed POPSI?
    (a) Ranganathan (b) G Bhattacharyya
    (c) Eugin Garfield (d) C.A Cutter
45. What is the chief source of information for a book?
    (a) Flap (b) Title page
    (c) Back of title page (d) Secret page

Answer : 38. (c) 39. (d) 40. (a) 41. (a) 42. (b)
43. (b) 44. (b) 45. (b)

46. What is 'tell-tale title?
    (a) Tale books
    (b) Title that discloses subject of a document
    (c) Sacred books
    (d) Reference book
47. Which type of reference entries are prepared, both referred from and referred to headings?
    (a) See (b) See also
    (c) Analytical entry (d) Series entry
48. British Museum Code was prepare by
    (a) A. Panizzi (b) Cutter
    (c) Brown (d) Sayers
49. If there are two authors for a book, how main entry will be prepared according to CCC?
    (a) First author only
    (b) Second author only
    (c) First and second authors
    (d) On title.
50. If a book is edited one, how main entry can be prepared according to CCC?
    (a) In the name of editor
    (b) In the name of title
    (c) In the name of publisher
    (d) In the name of series
51. In the case of more than two authors, how leading section of main entry can be prepared according to CCC?
    (a) First author & etal.
    (b) First and second author only
    (c) All authors
    (d) On title

Answer : 46. (b) 47. (a) 48. (a) 49. (c) 50. (a) 51. (a)

52. In the case of edited works, how leading section of main entry is to be prepared according to AACR-II?
    (a) On editor (b) On title
    (c) On series (d) On collaborator

53. In the case of more than three authors, what will come in leading section according to AACR-II?
    (a) Title
    (b) First author
    (c) First and second authors
    (d) All authors

54. Cross-reference entry is also called
    (a) Class index entry (b) Book index entry
    (c) Analytical entry
    (d) Subject analytical entry

55. Hierarchical relation in a thesaurus is a relation between
    (a) BT and RT (b) RT and BT
    (c) NT and RT (d) BT and NT

56. Science citation index was started by
    (a) Eugine Garfield (b) Derik Austin
    (c) Lancaster (d) Foskettc

57. In CCC, the name of the series in the main entry is rendered in
    (a) Title section (b) Heading section
    (c) Note section (d) Tracing section

58. In CCC, Class index entries are prepared for the .... only
    (a) Sought links (b) Unsought links
    (c) False links (d) Missing link

Answer : 52. (b) 53. (a) 54. (d) 55. (d) 56. (a)
57. (c) 58. (a)

59. The classified part of CCC consists of main entry and
    (a) Book index entry
    (b) Class index entry
    (c) Cross reference entry
    (d) Cross reference index entry
60. According to AAR-II physical description about a document in a catalogue entry is called
    (a) Collation
    (b) Imprint
    (c) Physical description
    (d) Additional useful information
61. According to AACR-II, publication details about a document in catalogue is called
    (a) Collation (b) Imprint
    (c) Physical description (d) None of the above
62. How many catalogue cards can be stored in a catalogue tray?
    (a) 1000 (b) 1500
    (c) 2000 (d) 2500
63. Full form of OPAC
    (a) Online Private Access Catalogue
    (b) Online Personal Access Catalogue
    (c) Offline Public Access Catalogue
    (d) Online Public Access Catalogue
64. COMPASS was introduced for
    (a) BNB (b) INB
    (c) ABPR (d) CIP

Answer : 59. (c) 60. (a) 61. (b) 62. (a) 63. (d) 64. (c)

65. Full form of CMPASS is
    (a) Computer Aided Subject System
    (b) Computer Aided Serial System
    (c) Computer Aided Service system
    (d) Common Awareness Subject System

Answer : 65. (a)

5. Information Science

1. RTI (Right to Information) Act was passed in India in which year?
   (a) 2001 (b) 2005
   (c) 2008 (d) 2010
2. Which is the real process of wisdom?
   (a) Data, information, knowledge, wisdom
   (b) Wisdom, information, knowledge, data
   (c) Data, wisdom, knowledge, information
   (d) Information, knowledge, data, wisdom
3. Who said that information is product and process both?
   (a) Ranganathan (b) Dewey
   (c) J. Martin (d) Foskette
4. What is knowledge?
   (a) Human thought
   (b) Human behavior
   (c) Organized body of information
   (d) Structured data
5. Information retrieval was first used in place of documentation by
   (a) H.P Luhn (b) Dewey
   (c) Ranganathan (d) Calvin Moores
6. The term bibliography was derived from
   (a) Latin (b) Greek
   (c) French (d) German

Answer : 1. (b) 2. (a) 3. (c) 4. (c) 5. (d) 6. (b)

7. Who used the word 'bibliography' first?
   (a) Ranganathan
   (b) Dewey
   (c) Louis Jacob De saint Charles
   (d) Calvin Moores
8. National bibliography is a list of
   (a) Books on a nation
   (b) Books published in a particular nation
   (c) Books written by a national government
   (d) Books of national library
9. Who divided sources of information in to three (primary, secondary and tertiary?)
   (a) Grogan (b) Dewey
   (c) Ranganathan (d) Sayers
10. National bibliography is which kind of source of information?
    (a) primary (b) Secondary
    (c) Tertiary (d) None of these
11. Bibliography of bibliographies is which kind of source of information?
    (a) Primary (b) Secondary
    (c) Tertiary (d) None of these
12. INB (Indian National Bibliography) was first published in which year
    (a) 1950 (b) 1952
    (c) 1957 (d) 1960
13. What is the periodicity of INB?
    (a) Weekly (b) Monthly
    (c) Fortnightly (d) Quarterly

Answer : 7. (c) 8. (b) 9. (a) 10(b) 11. (c) 12. (c) 13. (b)

14. BNB (British National Bibliography) was first published in which year?
    (a) 1950 (b) 1952
    (c) 1957 (d) 1960
15. What is the periodicity of BNB?
    (a) Weekly (b) Fortnightly
    (c) Monthly (d) bi-monthly
16. Which is the most popular encyclopedia in the world?
    (a) Encyclopaedia Britannica
    (b) Encyclopedia Americana
    (c) Encyclopedia Indiana
    (d) McGraw-Hill encyclopedia of Science & technology
17. Which one of the following is correctly spelled?
    (a) Encyclopedia Britannica
    (b) Encyclopaedia Britanica
    (c) Encyclopedia Britannica
    (d) Encyclopaedia Britannica
18. Which one of the following is correctly spelled?
    (a) Stateman Yearbook
    (b) Statesman yearbook
    (c) Statesman's Year book
    (d) Stateman's Year book
19. Chemical Abstract is published by?
    (a) Indian Chemical Society
    (b) American Chemical Society
    (c) British Chemical Society
    (d) Canadian Chemical Society

Answer : 14. (a) 15. (a) 16. (a) 17. (d) 18. (c) 19. (b)

20. What is the frequency of Chemical Abstract?
    (a) Weekly (b) Fortnightly
    (c) Monthly (d) Bi-monthly
21. Who publishes mathematical reviews?
    (a) Indian Mathematical Society
    (b) American Mathematical Society
    (c) British Mathematical Society
    (d) Canadian Mathematical Society
22. LISA (Library and Information Science Abstract) is published by
    (a) Library Association
    (b) Indian Library Association
    (c) American Library Association
    (d) INSDOC
23. 'Guide to Literature' is which kind of source of information?
    (a) Primary (b) Secondary
    (c) Tertiary (d) None of these
24. Research Journals are which type of source of information
    (a) Primary (b) Secondary
    (c) Tertiary (d) None of these
25. Translation of documents comes under which category of source of information?
    (a) Primary (b) Secondary
    (c) Tertiary (d) None of these
26. Routing of Journals is which kind of service?
    (a) Reference service
    (b) Referral service
    (c) Current Awareness Service
    (d) SDI

Answer : 20. (a) 21. (b) 22. (a) 23. (c) 24. (a) 25. (b) 26. (c)

27. The term SDI (Selective Dissemination of Information) was coined by
    (a) H.P Luhn (b) Calvin Moores
    (c) Foskette (d) Ranganathan
28. Feed back mechanism is one of the components of
    (a) CAS (b) SDI
    (c) Reference Service (d) Referral Service
29. SDI is which kind of service?
    (a) Current Awareness Service
    (b) Reference Service
    (c) Referral Service
    (d) Reprographic Service
30. In SDI service, user's profile is matched with
    (a) Document profile
    (b) Author's profile
    (c) Subject profile
    (d) None of these
31. INSDOC was established in which year
    (a) 1950 (b) 1952
    (c) 1957 (d) 1927
32. What is the present name of INSDOC?
    (a) NSSAT (b) NISCAIR
    (c) ICSSR (d) NISSCOM
33. The headquarters of NISCAIR is at
    (a) New Delhi (b) Mumbai
    (c) Hyderabad (d) Chennai

Answer : 27. (a) 28. (b) 29. (a) 30. (a) 31. (b) 32. (b) 33. (a)

34. What is the full form of NISCAIR?
    (a) National Institute of Science Communication and Information Resources
    (b) National Information Science Communication Resource Centre
    (c) National Institute of Social Science Communication Resource Centre
    (d) National Institute of Science Documentation centre

35. DESIDOC was established in which year?
    (a) 1952 (b) 1957
    (c) 1970 (d) 1972

36. SENDOC was established in which year?
    (a) 1970 (b) 1971
    (c) 1975 (d) 1980

37. Who sponsors NASSDOC?
    (a) ICSSR (b) CSIR
    (c) ICMR (d) ICAR

38. NASSDOC is situated at
    (a) New Delhi (b) Ahmedabad
    (c) Mumbai (d) Chennai

39. What does NASSDOC stands for?
    (a) National Social Science Documentation Centre
    (b) National Science Documentation
    (c) National Social Science Documentation
    (d) National Scientific Documentation Centre

Answer : 34. (a) 35. (c) 36. (b) 37. (a) 38. (a) 39. (a)

40. NISSAT stands for

(a) National Information System for Science & Technology

(b) National Information Service for Science & Technology

(c) National Institute of Social Science and Technology

(d) National Information Centre for Science and Technology

41. Where is PIS (Patent Information System) situated?

(a) New Delhi (b) Luck now

(c) Kanpur (d) Nagpur

42. *Indian Science Abstract* is published by

(a) NISCAIR (b) DESIDOC

(c) SENDOC (d) CSIR

43. Which is the International Information Storage and Retrieval System for Nuclear Science and Technology?

(a) AGRIS (b) NICNET

(c) INFLIBNET (d) INIS

44. What does INIS stands for

(a) Indian Nuclear Information System

(b) International Nuclear Information System

(c) Information Network of Information science

(d) Information Network of Information Systems

45. Indian input centre of INIS is

(a) INSDOC (b) NASSDOC

(c) SENDOC (d) BARC

Answer : 40. (a) 41. (d) 42. (a) 43. (d) 44. (b) 45. (d)

46. What is the full form of ENVIS?
   (a) Environmental Information Service
   (b) Energy Information Service
   (c) Engineering Information Service
   (d) Environment Information System
47. In which year DRTC (Documentation Research Training Centre) was established?
   (a) 1960 (b) 1962
   (c) 1963 (d) 1965
48. DRTC is located at
   (a) New Delhi (b) Bangalore
   (c) Hyderabad (d) Mysore
49. What does DEVSIS stands for
   (a) Department of Veterinary science Information Centre
   (b) Development Science Information System
   (c) Development of Veterinary Science
   (d) None of these
50. What is the full form of IAEA?
   (a) International Atomic Energy Academy
   (b) International Atomic Energy Agency
   (c) Indian Atomic Energy Agency
   (d) Indian Atomic Energy Academy
51. IAEA was established in which year
   (a) 1947 (b) 1950
   (c) 1952 (d) 1957
52. NASSDOC was established in which year?
   (a) 1947 (b) 1950
   (c) 1952 (d) 1969

Answer : 46. (a) 47. (b) 48. (b) 49. (b) 50. (b) 51. (d) 52. (d)

53. *World of Learning* falls under which category
    (a) Directory (b) Yearbook
    (c) Encyclopedia (d) Dictionary
54. *Science citation index* is a publication of
    (a) American Scientific Society
    (b) Institute of Scientific Information, Philadelphia
    (c) NISCAIR
    (d) ICSSR
55. *Library Literature* is a
    (a) Abstracting periodical
    (b) Indexing periodical
    (c) Yearbook
    (d) Encyclopedia
56. Who is the publisher of Library Literature?
    (a) RR Bowker
    (b) H.W Wilson
    (c) McGraw hill
    (d) University Press, London
57. *Dictionary of National Bibliography* is published by
    (a) RR Bowker, New York
    (b) H.W Wilson
    (c) Oxford
    (d) University Press, London
58. Who is the publisher of *world of learning?*
    (a) Europa, London (b) RR Bowker
    (c) H.W Wilson (d) McGraw Hill
59. Who is the publisher of *Books in Print?*
    (a) Europa, London (b) RR Bowker, New York
    (c) H.W Wilson (d) Whitaker

Answer : 53. (a) 54. (b) 55. (b) 56. (b) 57. (d) 58. (a) 59. (b)

60. To know the bibliographical details of a book, published in India, appropriate source is
    (a) Books in Print
    (b) Indian Books in Print
    (c) World of learning
    (d) Indian Books Directory
61. *Cumulative Book Index* is published by
    (a) H.W Wilson, New York
    (b) RR Bowker, New York
    (c) Whitaker, London
    (d) Europa, London
62. *Keesing's record of world event* is published from
    (a) London (b) New York
    (c) New Delhi (d) Philadelphia
63. What is the frequency of *Keesing's record of world events?*
    (a) Weekly (b) Fortnightly
    (c) Monthly (d) Quarterly
64. *Asian Recorder* is published from
    (a) London (b) Tokyo
    (c) New Delhi (d) Colombo
65. Who is the publisher of *Encyclopedia Americana*?
    (a) H.W Wilson (b) Bowker
    (c) Grolier (d) Europa
66. *New Encyclopaedia Britannica is* published from
    (a) London (b) New York
    (c) Chicago (d) Paris

Answer : 60. (b) 61. (a) 62. (a) 63. (c) 64. (c) 65. (c) 66. (c)

67. Who is the publisher of *Encyclopedia of Library Science?*

(a) Allen Kent (b) Marcel Decker
(c) H.W Wilson (d) RR.Bowker

68. Who is the editor of *Encyclopedia of Library Science?*

(a) Allen Kent & Harold Lancour
(b) Gullic & Urwick
(c) Faradaine
(d) Lancaster

69. *Book Review Digest* is published by

(a) H.W Wilson (b) R.R Bowker
(c) Europa (d) Keesings

70. *Library Trend* is published by

(a) Oxford University, London
(b) University of Illinois
(c) Chicago University
(d) Cambridge university

71. Abstracting and Indexing Periodicals come under which category

(a) Primary source (b) Secondary source
(c) Tertiary source (d) None of these

72. Union Catalogues comes under which category?

(a) Primary source (b) Secondary source
(c) Tertiary source (d) None of these

73. Old name of *South Asian Biographer*?

(a) South Asian Books
(b) List of South Asian Books
(c) Accession List of South Asia
(d) None of these

Answer : 67. (b) 68. (a) 69. (a) 70. (b) 71. (b) 72. (c) 73. (c)

74. *Roster of Indian Scientific and Technical Translator* is published by
    (a) NISCAIR (b) CSIR
    (c) ICSSR (d) DRTC
75. .... is the most suitable source for synonyms
    (a) Dictionaries (b) Encyclopedias
    (c) Thesaurus (d) Almanacs
76. *Poly got* is the name generally given to...
    (a) Bi-lingual Dictionaries
    (b) Multi-lingual Dictionaries
    (c) Bi-lingual Encyclopedias
    (d) Multi-lingual Encyclopedias
77. *Current Biography* is published by
    (a) H.W Wilson (b) RR Bowker
    (c) Europa (d) Grolier
78. Official announcement and Notification is available in which source of information?
    (a) News papers (b) Gazetteer
    (c) Gazette (d) Almanac
79. *Translationum Indicorum* is published by
    (a) ILA
    (b) National Library Calcutta
    (c) NISCAIR
    (d) IISc, Bangalore
80. *Index Translationum* is an annual catalogue of translations published by
    (a) ILA
    (b) National Library, Calcutta
    (c) UNESCO
    (d) UNO

Answer : 74. (a) 75. (c) 76. (b) 77. (a) 78. (c) 79. (b) 80. (c)

81. An alphabetical index to a book or an author's work is known as
    (a) Index (b) Bibliography
    (c) Concordance (d) Citation
82. The science of compiling a dictionary is called
    (a) Lexicology (b) Paleography
    (c) Calligraphy (d) Lexicography
83. Which of the following reference source is known as "backbone of reference service in libraries"?
    (a) Dictionaries (b) Encyclopedias
    (c) Atlas (d) Gazetteers
84. The first known encyclopedia was written by
    (a) Dewey (b) F.W Tailor
    (c) Aristotle (d) Plato
85. Words or phrases made by re-arranging the letter of another word or phrase is called
    (a) Synonym (b) Antonym
    (c) Acronym (d) Angram
86. *Indian books in print* is an example of which type of bibliography?
    (a) Trade (b) National
    (c) Universal (d) Academic
87. The CD-ROM version of Chemical Abstract was started I n which year?
    (a) 1998 (b) 1999
    (c) 2000 (d) 2003
88. The first edition of Encyclopedia Americana was published in
    (a) 1800 (b) 1817
    (c) 1829 (d) 1895

Answer : 81. (c) 82. (d) 83. (b) 84. (c) 85. (d) 86. (a) 87. (b) 88. (c)

89. *Universities handbook: India* is published by
    (a) University Grants Commission
    (b) Indian Library Association
    (c) Association of Indian Universities
    (d) Ministry of Human Resource
90. INPADOC (International Patent Documentation Centre) is situated at
    (a) London (b) New York
    (c) Washington DC (d) Vienna
91. *International Who is Who* is published by
    (a) RR Bowker (b) H.W Wilson
    (c) Europa (d) Oxford Press
92. *World Tables* is a publication of
    (a) UNESCO (b) World Bank
    (c) IMF (d) WHO
93. Keesing's record of world event is published in
    (a) Weekly (b) Monthly
    (c) Quarterly (d) Yearly
94. *Data India* is published by
    (a) PTI (b) Times of India
    (c) Door Darshan (d) Prasar Bharadi
95. Summary of world broadcast is published by
    (a) BBC (b) National Geographic
    (c) Door Darshan (d) CNN
96. The Universal Bibliographic Control (UB(C) programme sponsored by IFLA in the year
    (a) 1970 (b) 1973
    (c) 1974 (d) 1975

Answer : 89. (c) 90. (d) 91. (c) 92. (b) 93. (b) 94. (a) 95. (a) 96. (c)

97. Who coined the term 'Atlas' first?
    (a) Mercquator (b) Nasirudheen sha
    (c) Foskette (d) Brown
98. The fist model of globe was made in 1492 at
    (a) Luxemburg, Germany
    (b) Hiroshima
    (c) Mesopotamia, Egypt
    (d) Gujarat, India
99. The official mapping organization in India is
    (a) Survey of India
    (b) National Atlas organisation
    (c) Geological survey of India
    (d) Dept. of Geology
100. A geographical dictionary is
    (a) Gazette (b) Gazetteer
    (c) Atlas (d) Map
101. District gazetteers could be called as
    (a) Abridged encyclopedia
    (b) Miniature encyclopedia
    (c) Gazetteer encyclopedia
    (d) Encyclopedia of district
102. The number of volumes of new encyclopedia Britannica is
    (a) 12 (b) 20
    (c) 30 (d) 32
103. In which year the census started first?
    (a) 1872 (b) 1800
    (c) 1897 (d) 1900

Answer : 97. (a) 98. (a) 99. (c) 100. (b) 101. (b) 102. (c) 103. (a)

104. The best source to know the climate of kerala is
    (a) India: a reference annual
    (b) Gazetteer of India
    (c) Atlas of India
    (d) Gazette of Kerala

105. The best reference source to know the course details of Oxford University is
    (a) State's mans Yearbook
    (b) Europa yearbook
    (c) Universities Handbook
    (d) World of Learning

106. What is "Grey Literature"?
    (a) Digital form of literature
    (b) Document which is bound in grey cloth
    (c) Literature which is semi-published
    (d) Literature which will be published in future

107. The Concept of "Technological gate keepers" was first propounded by
    (a) Derik Austin (b) Dewey
    (c) Ranganathan (d) H.P Luhn

108. Encyclopaedia Britannica was started its publication in
    (a) 1768 (b) 1877
    (c) 1876 (d) 1800

109. In which year the first edition of Encyclopedia Americana was first published in?
    (a) 1800 (b) 1829
    (c) 1876 (d) 1877

Answer : 104. (b) 106. (c) 107. (a) 108. (a) 109. (b)

110. Encyclopedia of Library science was started in which year?
(a) 1876 (b) 1789
(c) 1929 (d) 1968

111. "A dictionary of Arts and Sciences" was the first name of which of the following?
(a) Oxford English Dictionary
(b) Encyclopaedia Britannica
(c) Encyclopedia Americana
(d) Encyclopedia of Social sciences

112. The first edition of Oxford English Dictionary was came out in
(a) 1789 (b) 1876
(c) 1857 (d) 1957

113. Who among the following categorized information into –conventional, non-conventional, neo-conventional and micro document?
(a) Hanson (b) Denis Grogan
(c) Ranganathan (d) Dewey

114. Who among the following categorized information in to primary, secondary and tertiary?
(a) Hanson (b) Denis Grogan
(c) Ranganathan (d) Dewey

115. Hanson divided the information source into how many categories?
(a) 2 (b) 3
(c) 4 (d) 5

Answer : 110. (d) 111. (b) 112. (c) 113. (c) 114. (b) 115. (a)

116. Which edition of *New encyclopaedia Britannica* is known Scholarly edition?
(a) 1st (b) 5
(c) 9 (d) 20

117. In how many parts New Encyclopaedia Britannica is published?
(a) 3 (b) 4
(c) 5 (d) 6

118. Encyclopedia Americana is published in how many volumes?
(a) 10 (b) 20
(c) 30 (d) 32

119. When the word 'information 'was first used?
(a) 1950 (b) 1955
(c) 1960 (d) 1965

Answer : 116. (c) 117. (a) 118. (c) 119. (c)

6. Information Technology

1. In which year 'Google' the most famous search engine was developed?
   (a) 2004 (b) 2005
   (c) 2001 (d) 2008
2. National Knowledge Commission was set up in?
   (a) 2001 (b) 2003
   (c) 2005 (d) 2008
3. In which year 'wikipedia' was developed?
   (a) 2000 (b) 2001
   (c) 2002 (d) 2003
4. Get into the website of a person / institution without permission is known as
   (a) Intruding (b) Pulling
   (c) Phishing (d) Hacking
5. Creating a website, look identical to the original site is known
   (a) Dupe siting (b) Hacking
   (c) Phishing (d) Hubbing
6. Odd one out
   (a) Windows (b) Dos
   (c) Photoshop (d) Linux
7. Odd one out
   (a) MacFe (b) PC Cilline
   (c) Avast (d) photoshop
8. Odd one out
   (a) Internet Explorer (b) Opera
   (c) Mozilla Fire fox (d) Linux

Answer : 1. (a) 2. (c) 3. (b) 4. (d) 5. (c) 6. (c) 7. (d) 8. (d)

9. Which is the internet browser, developed in India?
   (a) Epic (b) Opera
   (c) Indian (d) Mozilla Fire fox
10. Which is the Operating system developed by Google for mobile phone?
    (a) Opera (b) Apple
    (c) Android (d) Google phone
11. Who wrote the book '*A better India, a better world*'?
    (a) NR Narayana Moorthy
    (b) Visesarayya
    (c) Asim Premgi
    (d) Rattan Tata
12. Which is the place internet, where one can upload and download video files?
    (a) Website (b) You tube
    (c) Search engine (d) Explorer
13. Who is the present owner of Google?
    (a) Bill Gates (b) Ken Thomson
    (c) Irish Mitty (d) Vijay Mallya
14. What is the name of research centre, developed by Microsoft Corporation in Bangalore?
    (a) Microsoft research centre
    (b) Compusoft
    (c) Scientia
    (d) Operating research centre
15. Which is the world's first wireless internet country?
    (a) America (b) Japan
    (c) India (d) Mauritius

Answer : 9. (a) 10. (c) 11. (a) 12. (b) 13. (c) 14. (c) 15. (d)

16. Who is the father on Internet?
    (a) Bill Gates (b) Tim Berners Lee
    (c) Vint Cerf (d) Irish Mitty
17. Who developed 'Unix' operating system?
    (a) Ken Thomson (b) Irish Mitty
    (c) Vint Cerf (d) Tim Berners Lee
18. Who developed C++ programming language?
    (a) Ken Thomson (b) Irish Mitty
    (c) Byarne Stoustrup (d) Tim Berneslee
19. What is the full form of NIXI?
    (a) National Internet Exchange of Indian
    (b) National Information Exchange of India
    (c) National Internet Agency of India
    (d) National Information Agency of India
20. Who wrote the book "*The art of Computer Programming*"?
    (a) William Gibson (b) Donald Neuth
    (c) Ken Thomson (d) Bill Gates
21. Who used the term, "Cyber Space"?
    (a) William Gibson (b) Donald Neuth
    (c) Irish Mitty (d) Bill Gates
22. The damaged (unreadable) text file is called
    (a) Jung text (b) Cipher text
    (c) Waste text (d) Collapsed text
23. Microsoft- Office was developed in which year?
    (a) 1985 (b) 1989
    (c) 2001 (d) 1992

Answer : 16. (c) 17. (a) 18. (c) 19. (a) 20. (b)
21. (a) 22. (b) 23. (b)

24. World Animation day' is observed in which date?
    (a) Jan1 (b) Dec8
    (c) Oct 28 (d) Sept 13
25. Head quarters of 'Acer' company is at
    (a) London (b) Tokyo
    (c) Thai van (d) Paris
26. What is 'Webby'?
    (a) Oscar award in the internet
    (b) A person who became addict of internet
    (c) A person who fears Internet
    (d) Problem in using Internet
27. Which of the following types of memories is volatile?
    (a) RAM (b) ROM
    (c) PROM (d) WORM
28. Arithmetic and logic Unit (ALU) is a
    (a) Hardware (b) Software
    (c) Human ware (d) None of these
29. FORTRAN is a
    (a) Super Computer (b) High level language
    (c) Hardware (d) None of these
30. The device that converts digital to analog and analog to digital signals known as
    (a) Mobile phone (b) SMBS
    (c) Modem (d) CPU
31. Who among the following was the beginner of internet?
    (a) NICENET (b) ALANET
    (c) ARPANET (d) LISNET

Answer : 24. (c) 25. (c) 26. (a) 27. (a) 28. (a) 29. (b) 30. (c) 31. (c)

32. Binary system of numbers uses only
    (a) Two digits (b) Three digits
    (c) Four digits (d) Five digits
33. Which of the following is not a programming language?
    (a) C++ (b) COBOL
    (c) FORTRAN (d) ASCII
34. In computer terminology an error in a programme is known as
    (a) Bus (b) Bug
    (c) Virus (d) Error
35. The memory capacity of a computer is measured in
    (a) Bytes (b) Kilograms
    (c) Pages (d) Chips
36. In the binary system 100 represents the decimal number
    (a) 100 (b) 4
    (c) 2 (d) 1000
37. In relation to computer, COM means
    (a) Computer output microform
    (b) Catalogue on magnetic form
    (c) Computer output magnetic tape
    (d) Catalogue on microform
38. In relation to computer, BASIC is
    (a) Hardware
    (b) Basic components of computer
    (c) Programming language
    (d) Memory

Answer : 32. (a) 33. (d) 34. (b) 35. (a) 36. (b) 37. (a) 38. (c)

39. A byte normally denotes
    (a) String of four bits
    (b) String of six bits
    (c) String of eight bits
    (d) String of ten bits
40. Touch screen device is an example of
    (a) In put device (b) Out put device
    (c) Memory device (d) Controlling device
41. VDU (Visual Display Unit) is an example of
    (a) Input device (b) Output device
    (c) Memory device (d) Control device
42. IBM stands for
    (a) International Business Management
    (b) Indian Business Management
    (c) Indian Business Machine
    (d) International Business Machine
43. In machine format, the lowest unit of information is
    (a) Database (b) Data element
    (c) Field (d) Record
44. Which among the following is the highest unit of information?
    (a) KB (b) GB
    (c) TB (d) Bit
45. Logical operators, AND, OR, NOT are developed by
    (a) Alfred Bool (b) George Bool
    (c) Charles Babbage (d) Hawkins

Answer : 39. (c) 40. (a) 41. (b) 42. (d) 43. (b) 44. (c)

46. ENIAC Stands for
    (a) Electronic Numerical Integrator and Calculator
    (b) Electrified Numerical Integration and Calculator
    (c) Electronic Number Integrator and Calculator
    (d) Electrical Numerical Integrator and Calculator
47. UNIVAC stands for
    (a) United Nations Automatic Computer
    (b) Universal Automatic Computer
    (c) Union of World Computers
    (d) Universal computers.
48. DOS, LINUX, and Window are examples of
    (a) Application software
    (b) Operating systems
    (c) Hardware
    (d) Programming languages
49. Library software is an example of
    (a) System software (b) Language translators
    (c) Application software (d) Hardware
50. The components of a computer is
    (a) Input devices (b) Output devices
    (c) Central Processing Unit (d) All the above
51. Which of the following is a single- user operating system?
    (a) DOS (b) Windows
    (c) LINUX (d) UNIX
52. Who designed analytical engine?
    (a) Charles Babbage (b) Hawkins
    (c) Pascal (d) Gibson

Answer : 45. (b) 46. (a) 47. (b) 48. (b) 49. (c)
50. (d) 51. (a) 52. (a)

53. When computer was first applied in India?
    (a) 1947 (b) 1950
    (c) 1957 (d) 1985
54. Which agency used computer first in India?
    (a) INSDOC (b) BARC
    (c) ISRO (d) ISI, Calcutta
55. When CD-ROM was developed?
    (a) 1957 (b) 1962
    (c) 1985 (d) 1989
56. Full form of BASIC?
    (a) Basic All Purpose Symbolic Information Code
    (b) Beginners All Purpose Symbolic Instruction Code
    (c) Beginners All Purpose Symbolic Information Code
    (d) Basic Computers
57. What is the natural language of computer?
    (a) Computer language
    (b) Machine language
    (c) Spoken language
    (d) Programming language
58. What is called for a measure of amount of information that can be transmitted through internet?
    (a) Band (b) Bandwidth
    (c) Byte (d) Bit
59. IC Chips used in computers are made of?
    (a) Iron (b) Lead
    (c) Silicone (d) Gold

Answer : 53. (c) 54. (d) 55. (c) 56. (b) 57. (c) 58. (b) 59. (c)

60. One kilobyte is equal to
   (a) 100 bytes (b) 1000 bytes
   (c) 1024 bytes (d) 1024 bits

61. Which of the following is not an operating system?
   (a) Windows 2003 (b) Ms- Office
   (c) Redhat Linux (d) BSD UNIX

62. Which super computer is developed by Indian scientists?
   (a) Param (b) Super 301
   (c) CRAY YMP (d) Compaq Presario

63. The errors that can be pointed out by the complier are
   (a) Syntax error (b) Symantic error
   (c) Logical error (d) Internal error

64. What is the control unit's function in CPU?
   (a) To transfer data to primary storage
   (b) To store programme instructions
   (c) To perform logic functions
   (d) To interprets programme instructions & direct to execute

65. What do you use to create a chart in the computer?
   (a) Pie wizard (b) Excel wizard
   (c) Data wizard (d) Chart wizard

66. Which of the following command is given to re-boot the computer?
   (a) Cntl + Alt +Del (b) Cntl + Alt + Tab
   (c) Cntl + Shift + Del (d) Cntl + Shift + Alt

Answer : 60. (c) 61. (b) 62. (a) 63. (a) 64. (??) 65. (d) 66. (a)

67. The full form of ATM is
    (a) Any time Money
    (b) Automatic Marketing
    (c) Automatic Machine
    (d) Automatic Teller Machine
68. *Silicon valley of India* is called for
    (a) New Delhi (b) Bangalore
    (c) Mysore (d) Hyderabad
69. Computer code for interchange of information between terminals
    (a) ASCII (b) BSO
    (c) BCD (d) Hollerith
70. What is the brain of a computer?
    (a) CPU (b) Monitor
    (c) Keyboard (d) Mouse
71. Who wrote the book "*Computer Liberation and Dream Machine*"?
    (a) John Mc Carthy (b) Ted Nelson
    (c) Karl Capek (d) N.R Narayanamoorthy
72. Which is /are the main provision of IT Act 2000?
    (a) Finalisation of contracts through electronic media
    (b) Legal recognition to digital signatures and documents
    (c) Making hacking with computer system an office
    (d) All the above
73. PASCAL was developed by
    (a) John Mc Carthy (b) Niklaus Wirth
    (c) Karl Capek (d) William Gibson

Answer : 67. (d) 68. (b) 69. (a) 70. (a) 71. (b)
72. (d) 73. (b)

74. MS-DOS was developed in which year
    (a) 1957 (b) 1975
    (c) 1981 (d) 1985
75. Micro-Soft Windows was release in which year
    (a) 1993 (b) 1995
    (c) 2003 (d) 1985
76. In which year Linux was developed?
    (a) 1992 (b) 1985
    (c) 1995 (d) 1998
77. In which year Unix was developed?
    (a) 1969 (b) 1971
    (c) 1975 (d) 1985
78. 'BASIC' programming language was developed by
    (a) John George Kemeney
    (b) Dennis Ritchie
    (c) William Gibson
    (d) Ken Thomson
79. BASIC was developed in which year?
    (a) 1962 (b) 1970
    (c) 1964 (d) 1985
80. Programming language 'C' was developed by
    (a) John Kemeney (b) Ken Thomson
    (c) William Gibson (d) Dennis Ritchie
81. In which year C language was developed?
    (a) 1972 (b) 1975
    (c) 1985 (d) 1969

Answer : 74. (c) 75. (d) 76. (a) 77. (b) 78. (a)
79. (c) 80. (d) 81. (a)

82. Programming language 'Java' was developed by whom?
    (a) James Glosing (b) William Gibson
    (c) Dennis Ritchie (d) Byrne Stoustrap
83. Java was developed in which year?
    (a) 1975 (b) 1985
    (c) 1992 (d) 1995

Answer : 82. (a) 83. (d)

Part-3 : Solved Question Papers of Recent Competitive Examinations ...

1. Test for Librarian (Common pool), conducted by Public Service Commission-Kerala, March 2010.

2. Test for Librarian for Aryavidya Sala Research Centre, conducted by LBS Kerala in 2009.

3. Test for Librarian grade-3 for IHRD, conducted by LBS centre for science and technology in 2009.

4. Test for Librarian Grade-4, Conducted by Public Service Commission-Kerala in 2008.

5. UGC –National Eligibility Test of Library & Information Science –June 2010.

6. UGC – National Eligibility Test of Library & Information Science-Dec 2009.

7. UGC – National Eligibility Test of Library & Information Science – Dec 2008.

8. UGC – National Eligibility Test of Library & Information Science- June-2008.

PUBLIC SERVICE COMMISSION-KERALA

Examination for Librarian (Common pool)

March 2010

1. Where is the headquarters of ALA?
   (a) Chicago
   (b) Washington
   (c) Florida
   (d) Philadelphia
2. Which of the following is an international organization?
   (a) KLA
   (b) ILA
   (c) IFLA
   (d) BLA
3. COMLA stands for
   (a) Commission for Library Associations
   (b) Commonwealth countries Library Association
   (c) Cooperative movement of Library Authorities
   (d) Commonwealth Library Association
4. Which is the quarterly journal of ILA?
   (a) ILA Journal
   (b) ILA Bulletin
   (c) Library Literature
   (d) Quarterly of ILA
5. Which one of the following is the special library association of India?
   (a) IATLIS
   (b) ASLIB
   (c) IASLIC
   (d) SLA

Answer : 1. (a) 2. (c) 3. (d) 4. (b) 5. (c)

6. IFLA stands for
   (a) Indian Federation of Library Associations
   (b) International federation of library associations and institutions.
   (c) International fund for library associations
   (d) Indian film libraries Associations
7. Model Library Act was prepared by
   (a) UNESCO (b) S.R Ranganathan
   (c) ILA (d) IASIC
8. The National library of India receives books under
   (a) Delivery of Books Act, 1954
   (b) The Copyright Act, 1985
   (c) Registration of Books Act, 1887
   (d) Revision Act, 1976
9. Kerala Public library Act was enacted in
   (a) 1979 (b) 1996
   (c) 1989 (d) 1999
10. Library cess is levied in Kerala along with
    (a) Road tax (b) Building tax
    (c) Property tax (d) Wealth tax
11. POSDCORB formula was devised by
    (a) Gullick and Urvick (b) Ranganathan
    (c) Henry Fayol (d) Edward Evans
12. The term scientific management was coined by
    (a) F.W Taylor (b) Henry Fayol
    (c) Louis Brandies (d) M.C Clovin
13. Human behavior in management is related to
    (a) Social System
    (b) Human relation school
    (c) Classical school
    (d) Decision making system

Answer : 6. (b) 7. (b) 8. (a) 9. (c) 10. (b) 11. (a) 12. (a) 13. (b)

14. Library authority means
    (a) Governing Body (b) Librarian
    (c) Library users (d) Publishers
15. Evaluation of any library and information centre consists of Macro evaluation and
    (a) Micro evaluation (b) Exhaustive evaluation
    (c) Both A and B (d) None of the above
16. Budge of libraries is prepared for the
    (a) Current year (b) Past year
    (c) Next year (d) None of the above
17. What is budget?
    (a) Annual estimate of the expenditure
    (b) Annual estimate of income
    (c) Annual estimate of income and expenditure
    (d) Annual income and expenditure
18. What is recurring expenditure in the library budget?
    (a) Expenditure on books
    (b) Expenditure on staff salaries
    (c) Expenditure of stationary
    (d) Other expenditure
19. Zero-based budget means
    (a) No increase in income
    (b) No increase in expenditure
    (c) The expenses are zero
    (d) Budgeting afresh

Answer : 14. (a) 15. (a) 16. (c) 17. (c) 18. (b) 19. (d)

20. Annual report a library is prepared for informing
    (a) The authorities of libraries
    (b) The library staff
    (c) The users of the library
    (d) The general public
21. Annual report of library deals with
    (a) Account of the current year
    (b) Report of the current year
    (c) Report of the past year
    (d) Account of the past year
22. The main record of a library is
    (a) Budget (b) Annual report
    (c) Catalogue (d) Accession register
23. The secretary of library committee in an academic library is an example of
    (a) The vice-chancellor (b) The Registrar
    (c) The Librarian (d) The Finance officer
24. Management of the library by committee is an example of
    (a) Participative management
    (b) Decentralization
    (c) M.B.O
    (d) MIS
25. MIS stands for
    (a) Missing information service
    (b) Management information system
    (c) Management of information society
    (d) Mass information system

Answer : 20. (a) 21. (c) 22. (d) 23. (c) 24. (a) 25. (b)

26. The demand theory of book selection was coined by

    (a) Dewey (b) Ranganathan
    (c) McClovin (d) Bradford

27. The most popular system of circulation in libraries is

    (a) System analysis (b) New York system
    (c) Browney system (d) Register system

28. The Newark system is related to

    (a) Cataloguing (b) Book selection
    (c) Classification (d) Circulation

29. The main source of income for public libraries in Kerala is

    (a) UGC (b) State Govt.
    (c) Library cess (d) Library tax

30. Good Office Committee (GO(C) helps in determining

    (a) Book available in the market
    (b) Foreign exchange rate
    (c) Names of vendors
    (d) Names of publishers

31. Name the primary source of information

    (a) Union catalogue
    (b) Current content list
    (c) State of the art report
    (d) Manuscript

32. Identify the primary document

    (a) Bibliography (b) Directory
    (c) Dictionary (d) Research report

Answer : 26. (c) 27. (c) 28. (d) 29. (c) 30. (b) 31. (d) 32. (d)

33. Note down the secondary source of information
    (a) Patent (b) Standard
    (c) Abstracting periodical (d) Research report
34. Article published in research journals are
    (a) Reference source (b) Primary source
    (c) Secondary source (d) Tertiary source
35. Identify a tertiary document
    (a) Research paper
    (b) Thesis
    (c) List of abstracting service
    (d) Index
36. British National Bibliography is a
    (a) Primary source (b) Secondary source
    (c) Tertiary source (d) None
37. New Encyclopedia Britannica is published from
    (a) New York (b) London
    (c) Paris (d) Chicago
38. The publisher of encyclopedia Americana is
    (a) Marcel Decker (b) Grolier
    (c) McGraw Hill (d) Colliers
39. The author of 'The Da Vinici Code'
    (a) T.S Eliot (b) Dan Brown
    (c) Kiran Desai (d) Sidney Sheldon
40. India :a reference annual is an example of
    (a) Directory (b) Handbook
    (c) Year book (d) Statistical source

Answer : 33. (c) 34. (b) 35. (c) 36. (b) 37. (d) 38. (b) 39. (b) 40. (c)

41. Publisher of 'Universities Handbook: India'
    (a) National Book Trust
    (b) UGC
    (c) Association of Indian Universities
    (d) ILA
42. The place publication of Asian Recorder
    (a) Delhi (b) Tokyo
    (c) Kolkata (d) Peeking
43. Periodicity of Keesing's Record of world event
    (a) Weekly (b) Fortnightly
    (c) Monthly (d) Quarterly
44. Originator of the computer based SDI
    (a) Mortimer Taub (b) Garfield
    (c) H.P Luhn (d) B.C Vickery
45. INFLIBNET is a program of
    (a) CSIR (b) INSDOC
    (c) NISSAT (d) UGC
46. University library network in India
    (a) DELNET (b) CALIBNET
    (c) INFLIBNET (d) NICNET
47. The biggest network system in the world
    (a) EURONET (b) INFLIBNET
    (c) SIRNET (d) OCLC
48. ERNET is a project of
    (a) UGC
    (b) Department of Electronics
    (c) CSIR
    (d) Department of Education

Answer : 41. (c) 42. (a) 43. (c) 44. (c) 45. (d)
46. (c) 47. (d) 48. (b)

49. LAN stands for
    (a) Library and Network
    (b) Local Area Network
    (c) Library Automation Network
    (d) Library Associations Network

50. The use of library can be maximized
    (a) Application of computers
    (b) User Education
    (c) Reference service
    (d) Current Awareness service

51. OPAC stands for
    (a) Online Processing of Automated Catalogue
    (b) Online Public Access Catalogue
    (c) Online Program of Analog computer
    (d) Online Programming And Control

52. The means to bring together the related document of same subject at one place is
    (a) Indexing (b) Cataloguing
    (c) Classification (d) Documentation

53. APUPA stands for
    (a) Arunachal Pradesh University Players Association
    (b) Andhra Pradesh University Publication Academy
    (c) Alien Penumbral Umbral Penumbral Alien
    (d) Australian Public Utility Providers Association

54. Who is the author of Prolegomena to Classification?
    (a) Melvil Dewey (b) S.R Ranganathan
    (c) H.E Bliss (d) C.A Cutter

Answer : 49. (b) 50. (b) 51. (b) 52. (c) 53. (c) 54. (b)

55. Bio-tehnology is an example of generation of knowledge by
   (a) Fission (b) Fusion
   (c) Lamination (d) Loose Assemblage
56. The oldest classification scheme
   (a) UDC (b) DDC
   (c) EC (d) CC
57. The deviser of DDC was
   (a) Dewey (b) Ranganathan
   (c) Bliss (d) Sayers
58. A fully enumerative Classification scheme
   (a) Library of Congress
   (b) Expansive classification
   (c) Rider's International
   (d) Dewey decimal classification
59. 7th edition of CC is
   (a) An enumerative scheme
   (b) A fully faceted scheme
   (c) An almost faceted scheme
   (d) Almost enumerative scheme.
60. Basic structure of main class in UDC is based on
   (a) CC (b) LC
   (c) DDC (d) None of the above
61. The most difficult fundamental category to identify is
   (a) Personality (b) Matter
   (c) Energy (d) Time

Answer : 55. (b) 56. (b) 57. (a) 58. (a) 59. (b)
60. (c) 61. (a)

62. Classified Catalogue code (CC(C) was devised by
    (a) A. Panizzi (b) S.R Ranganathan
    (c) C.A Cutter (d) Melvil Dewey
63. The chief source of information for cataloguing a book is
    (a) Half title page (b) Back of title page
    (c) Title page (d) Book jacket
64. Ranganathan's chain procedure is meant for
    (a) Classification
    (b) Cataloguing
    (c) Abstracting
    (d) Deriving subject heading
65. POPSI is a
    (a) Post coordinate indexing system
    (b) Pre coordinates indexing system
    (c) Citation index
    (d) Key word indexing system
66. Science citation index was started by
    (a) Vickery (b) Foskett
    (c) Garfield (d) Lancaster
67. A referral centre provides
    (a) Required information directly
    (b) Abstracting service
    (c) Document delivery
    (d) No information directly but suggests sources
68. Notification of new arrivals of a special library is a
    (a) SDI service (b) Reference service
    (c) CAS service (d) Referral service

Answer : 62. (b) 63. (c) 64. (d) 65. (b) 66. (c) 67. (d) 68. (c)

69. In information service, SDI stands for
    (a) Selected Design of Information
    (b) Selective Dissemination of Information
    (c) Systematic Development of Information
    (d) Selected Development of Information
70. In SDI, document profile is matched with
    (a) Data base (b) Author's profile
    (c) Library software (d) User profile
71. INSDOC comes under
    (a) CSIR (b) UNESCO
    (c) UNISIST (d) NISSAT
72. Activities of SENDOC comes under
    (a) Science (b) Technology
    (c) Social science (d) Small enterprises
73. The parent body of DESIDCO is
    (a) CSIR (b) DRDO
    (c) NISSAT (d) ICSSR
74. NASSDOC comes under
    (a) ICMR (b) CSIR
    (c) ICAR (d) ICSSR
75. ENVIS stands for
    (a) Environmental International Society
    (b) Environmental Insurance System
    (c) Environmental Information Service
    (d) Entrepreneurial Information System
76. In CDS/ISIS, FDT stands for
    (a) Field Development Table
    (b) Field Definition Table
    (c) Field Declaration Table
    (d) Facet Definition Tool

Answer : 69. (b) 70. (d) 71. (a) 72. (d) 73. (b)
74. (d) 75. (c) 76. (b)

77. The language in which CDS/ISIS written is
(a) FORTRAN (b) COBOL
(c) PASCAL (d) PROLOG

78. CHECKMATE software package is used for
(a) Reference service (b) Acquisition of books
(c) Serial control (d) Information retrieval

79. Barcode labels are used in the
(a) Acquisition system (b) Circulation system
(c) Classification system (d) Serial control system

80. LIBSYS is software for
(a) Tourism (b) Libraries
(c) Hospital (d) Insurance

81. Micro CDS/ISIS is
(a) Menu driven package
(b) Information package
(c) Command driven package
(d) Computer directing system

82. A set of programmes for computer is
(a) Memory (b) Hardware
(c) Software (d) Brain ware

83. WWW stands for
(a) Waste Water Works
(b) Wide World Web
(c) World Wide Web
(d) Western Wireless World

84. Medical literature analysis and retrieval system is known as
(a) MLARS (b) MEDLARS
(c) MELIAN (d) MEDILIT

Answer : 77. (c) 78. (c) 79. (b) 80. (b) 81. (a)
82. (c) 83. (c) 84. (b)

85. INSPEC is a database in
    (a) International peace
    (b) Planning and development
    (c) Indian spices
    (d) Physics and electronics
86. AGRIS is a database of
    (a) UNESCO (b) FAO
    (c) UNIDO (d) ASIAN
87. The first step in library automation is
    (a) Data entry
    (b) Purchasing of software
    (c) System analysis
    (d) Purchasing of computer
88. Identify an housekeeping operation in library
    (a) Retrospective search (b) Serial control
    (c) SDI (d) CAS
89. KWIC falls under
    (a) Classification (b) Reference service
    (c) Abstracting (d) Indexing
90. ISBD is based on
    (a) CCC (b) AACR
    (c) MEDLARS (d) CDS/ISIS
91. Common Communication Format (CCF) was launched by
    (a) ALA (b) FID
    (c) UNIDO (d) UNESCO

Answer : 85. (d) 86. (b) 87. (c) 88. (b) 89. (d) 90. (b) 91. (d)

92. HTML stands for
    (a) Higher Texts and Manuals for Libraries
    (b) Hypertext Markup Language
    (c) Hyper Tools for Machine Language
    (d) Hotmail Technique for Many Letters
93. UNIX is a
    (a) Hardware (b) Operating system
    (c) High level language (d) Application software
94. The most popular use of internet is
    (a) Web hosting (b) E-commerce
    (c) E-mail (d) E-learning
95. International information system in Nuclear science is
    (a) NATIS (b) IISN
    (c) IISNS (d) INIS
96. Five laws of library science was developed by
    (a) Melvil Dewey (b) S.C Bradford
    (c) S.R Ranganathan (d) D.J Foskett
97. Which law of library science is related to the growth of the library?
    (a) First (b) Second
    (c) Fourth (d) Fifth
98. Which law of library science emphasizes the obligation of state to enact library legislation?
    (a) First (b) Second
    (c) Third (d) Fifth
99. Library week in India is observed every year during
    (a) 26th Jan to 2nd feb (b) 14th Nov to 20th Nov
    (c) 2nd Oct to 8th Oct (d) 15th Aug to 21st Aug

---

Answer : 92. (b) 93. (b) 94. (c) 95. (d) 96. (c) 97. (d) 98. (b) 99. (b)

100. What is the full name of ILA?

(a) International Library Association

(b) International Library Academy

(c) Indian Library Association

(d) Informal Library Association.

Answer : 100. (c)

Test of Librarian for Aryavidysala Research Centre By LBS Kerala 2009

1. NISCAIR stands for
   (a) National Information System Centre and Information Research
   (b) Nation Institute for Science Collection and Information Resources
   (c) National Information System for Communication and Information
   (d) National Institute for Science Communication and Information Resources
2. Who among the following is considered as the 'father of scientific management'?
   (a) F.W Taylor (b) Henry Fayol
   (c) Peter Drucker (d) Douglas McGregor
3. National Centre for science Information (NCSI) is located at
   (a) New Delhi (b) Kolkatta
   (c) Bangalore (d) Baroda
4. PRECIS was developed by
   (a) S.R Ranganathan (b) G Bhattacharyya
   (c) Derik Austin (d) E.J Coates
5. The Indian input centre to the AGRIS database is
   (a) BARC (b) CFTRI
   (c) ICAR (d) IARI
6. The functions of management as embodied in the acronym of POSDCORB was developed by
   (a) Maslow and McGregore
   (b) Maslow and Taylor
   (c) Gullick & Urvick
   (d) Mayo & McGregor

Answer : 1. (d) 2. (a) 3. (c) 4. (c) 5. (c) 6. (c)

7. The headquarters of International Serial Data System (ISDS) is at
   (a) New Delhi (b) Paris
   (c) Geneva (d) New York
8. Medline Database is created by
   (a) National library of Medicine, US
   (b) British Medical library
   (c) Indian Medical library
   (d) Medical library of France
9. *Chemical Abstracts,* the biggest abstracting periodical, has 80 parts under .....Sections
   (a) Five (b) Three
   (c) Four (d) Six
10. The 'web of knowledge' is the service offered by
    (a) BIOSIS (b) Pergamon
    (c) Elsevier (d) Thomson-ISI
11. *World of learning* is published by
    (a) Europa (b) Penguin
    (c) R.R Bowker (d) H.W Wilson
12. The term 'bibliometrics' was coined by
    (a) S.R Ranganathan (b) Alan Prichard
    (c) J.H Shera (d) Cole & Yales
13. *Universities handbook* is brought out by
    (a) Association of Indian Universities
    (b) Association of Commonwealth Universities
    (c) University Grants Commission
    (d) Europa publications

Answer : 7. (b) 8. (a) 9. (a) 10. (d) 11. (a) 12. (b) 13. (a)

14. Which one of the following is a British network?
    (a) DELNET (b) Super JANET
    (c) UUNET (d) ERNET
15. Which of the following is not application software?
    (a) Word (b) Linux
    (c) CDS/ISIS (d) Access
16. The headquarters of DEVSIS is at
    (a) Geneva (b) Munich
    (c) Ottawa (d) New York
17. Call number of a book consists of
    (a) Class number and book number
    (b) Class number and collection number
    (c) Class number, book number and collection number
    (d) Class number, book number and accession number
18. FRBR was initiated by
    (a) IFLA (b) FID
    (c) OCLC (d) LC
19. *Who's who of Indian writers* is a publication of
    (a) Kerala sahitya academy
    (b) Sahitya academy, New Delhi
    (c) National library, Kolkatta
    (d) Publication Division, Govt. of India
20. Which of the following database is available free through internet?
    (a) Excerpta medica (b) INIS
    (c) Medline (d) BIOSIS previews

Answer : 14. (b) 15. (b) 16. (c) 17. (c) 18. (a) 19. (b) 20. (c)

21. The term 'grey literature' refers to
    (a) Publication with grey cover
    (b) Publication not available through normal trade channels
    (c) Non-Print publications
    (d) Classified publications
22. ASLIB, the British professional association, is now known as
    (a) Association for Information Management
    (b) Association of Libraries
    (c) Association of Libraries and Information Bureaus
    (d) Association of State Libraries
23. The first edition of Colon Classification was published in
    (a) 1931 (b) 1932
    (c) 1933 (d) 1934
24. Three Card system was developed by S.R Ranganathan for
    (a) Issue of Books
    (b) Issue of Journals
    (c) Recording and receipt of books
    (d) Serial control
25. Which of the following is the most active network in India?
    (a) CALIBNET (b) BONET
    (c) DELNET (d) MALIBNET

Answer : 21. (b) 22. (a) 23. (c) 24. (d) 25. (c)

26. The counterpart of common isolate of CC in DDC is

(a) Area notation (b) Standard subdivision
(c) Common auxiliaries (d) Relative index

27. When was Raja Ram Mohan Roy Library Foundation established?

(a) 1966 (b) 1970
(c) 1972 (d) 1976

28. Which of the following law deals with productivity of authors?

(a) Lotka's law (b) Zip's law
(c) Bradoford's law (d) Garfield's law

29. How many Indian state have enacted library legislation so far

(a) 10 (b) 12
(c) 15 (d) 18

30. The title of the journal published by RRLF is

(a) Granthalaya (b) Granthana
(c) Granthasooji (d) Grantha loka

31. Who of the following put forward the concept of 'paperless society'?

(a) B.C Brookes (b) B.C Vickery
(c) D.J Foskett (d) F.W Lancaster

32. OCLC stands for

(a) Online Catalogue of Library of Congress
(b) Ohio College Library Computer
(c) Online College Library Centre
(d) Online Computer Library Centre

Answer : 26. (b) 27. (c) 28. (a) 29. (d) 30. (b)
31. (d) 32. (d)

33. Which of the following is not an example of a special library?
    (a) Prison library
    (b) Newspaper library
    (c) Polytechnic library
    (d) Government department library
34. National science library in India is located at
    (a) New Delhi (b) Kolkatta
    (c) Chennai (d) Mumbai
35. Which of the following is a library science journal published from India?
    (a) Journal of documentation
    (b) Library resources and technical services
    (c) SRELS journal
    (d) Library trends
36. The national library of USA is
    (a) Washington public library
    (b) New York public library
    (c) Library of Congress
    (d) American library
37. The 'Delivery of Books Act' in India was passed in the year
    (a) 1954 (b) 1956
    (c) 1947 (d) 1961
38. Former British library lending division is now known as
    (a) British library document supply centre
    (b) British library bibliographic division
    (c) British library research division
    (d) British library division for library co-operation

Answer : 33. (c) 34. (a) 35. (c) 36. (c) 37. (a) 38. (a)

39. The latest revision of 'UNESCO public library manifesto' came out in
    (a) 1948 (b) 1974
    (c) 1994 (d) 2004
40. Which of the following is DTP software?
    (a) Page Maker (b) Access
    (c) Excel (d) Power Point
41. *Indian science abstract* brought by
    (a) NISCAIR (b) DESIDOC
    (c) NISTADS (d) ICAR
42. An Almanac in its content is closer to
    (a) Directory (b) Year book
    (c) Encyclopaedia (d) Handbook
43. The number of volumes of 2nd edition of *Oxford English Dictionary* is
    (a) Ten (b) Twelve
    (c) Twenty (d) Twenty four
44. The first scientific journal is
    (a) Transactions of philosophical society
    (b) Journal of royal society
    (c) Proceedings of Smithsonian society
    (d) Journal of the Asiatic society
45. NUCSSI is the catalogue of
    (a) Social science journals
    (b) Science journals
    (c) Sociology journals
    (d) Chemical science journals

Answer : 39. (c) 40. (a) 41. (a) 42. (b) 43. (c) 44. (a) 45. (b)

46. *Guide to Indian Periodical literature* is published from

    (a) New Delhi (b) Bangalore

    (c) Jaipur (d) Gurgaon

47. The periodicity of *Indian National Bibliography* is

    (a) Monthly (b) Bi-monthly

    (c) Quarterly (d) Annual

48. Which of the following source can be consulted to know about the circulation of the periodicals?

    (a) Ulrich's periodicals directory

    (b) Indian periodicals directory

    (c) World list of periodicals

    (d) Serials of the world

49. *India :a reference annual* is published by

    (a) Ministry of Human Resource Development

    (b) Ministry of Information and Broadcasting

    (c) Ministry of Communication

    (d) Planning Commission

50. The new name of former *kessings Contemporary Archives* is

    (a) Kessing's record of contemporary events

    (b) Kessing's record of Global events

    (c) Kessing's record of recent events

    (d) Kessing's record of World events

51. 'SOUL' library software is developed by

    (a) INSDOC (b) DESIDOC

    (c) SENDOC (d) INFLIBNET

Answer : 46. (d) 47. (a) 48. (a) 49. (b) 50. (d) 51. (d)

52. The on-line union catalogue of OCLC is known as
    (a) Copy cat (b) World cat
    (c) First cat (d) Union cat
53. Which of the following is a database in Medicine?
    (a) DEVSIS (b) dBASE
    (c) EMBASE (d) MEDBASE
54. The headquarters of FID is
    (a) Geneva (b) Vienna
    (c) London (d) Hague
55. Which of the following classification scheme is published as a British standard?
    (a) DDC (b) UDC
    (c) CC (d) BC
56. A work of unknown or doubtful authorship is referred to as
    (a) Pseudonymous work
    (b) Eponymous work
    (c) Anonymous work
    (d) Author merged with title
57. *Chemical abstracts* was started in the year?
    (a) 1907 (b) 1910
    (c) 1922 (d) 1927
58. Which of the following classification scheme contains the rules for constructing book numbers?
    (a) UDC (b) DDC
    (c) RIC (d) CC
59. 'Universal availability of publication' (UAP) was a programme of
    (a) UNESCO (b) IFLA
    (c) FID (d) FAO

Answer : 52. (b) 53. (c) 54. (d) 55. (b) 56. (c) 57. (a) 58. (d) 59. (b)

60. The 'Press and Registration of Books Act' was enforced in India
    (a) 1970 (b) 1954
    (c) 1867
61. Systematic training on librarianship was initiated in Baroda by
    (a) W.A Bordon (b) Asa Don Dickinson
    (c) John McFarlane (d) S.R Ranganathan
62. Mobile library service is very often offered by
    (a) Academic libraries (b) National libraries
    (c) Special libraries (d) Public libraries
63. In Colon Classification, the ordinal value of "sigma" (social science) is between
    (a) S and T (b) L and M
    (c) R and S (d) T and U
64. 'A digit with ordinal value but without a semantic value' is called
    (a) Spectator (b) Connecting digit
    (c) Empty digit (d) Emptying digit
65. The 'demand theory of book selection' was put forward by
    (a) Dewey (b) Drury
    (c) McClovin (d) Ranganathan
66. The Kerala public libraries Act was passed in which year?
    (a) 1975 (b) 1994
    (c) 1985 (d) 1989
67. The expansion of ERNET is
    (a) Electronic and Research Network
    (b) Education and Research Network
    (c) Educational Resource Network
    (d) Electronic Resource Network

Answer : 60. (c) 61. (a) 62. (d) 63. (a) 64. (c) 65. (c) 66. (d) 67. (b)

68. Colon Classification devises the class number of a 'system facet' using
    (a) Geographical device (b) Chronological device
    (c) Enumeration device (d) Phase Device
69. Which of the following is not a trade catalogue?
    (a) Books in Print
    (b) Accession list: South Asia
    (c) Book Bank CD-ROM
    (d) Publishers trade list annual
70. The kind of 'mnemonics' not used in Colon Classification is
    (a) Verbal mnemonics
    (b) Seminal mnemonics
    (c) Scheduled mnemonics
    (d) National mnemonics
71. *Indian library science abstract* is brought by
    (a) ILA (b) IASIC
    (c) NISCAIR (d) DESIDOC
72. The 'need theory' (hierarchy of human needs) was put forward
    (a) McGregor (b) Drucker
    (c) Fayol (d) Maslow
73. *Annual review of Information science and Technology* is published by
    (a) Marcel Decker (b) Bowker
    (c) Libraries unlimited (d) Information today, Inc
74. The International Standard Book Number (ISBN) now has ..... digits
    (a) 10 (b) 8
    (c) 12 (d) 13

Answer : 68. (b) 69. (b) 70. (d) 71. (b) 72. (d) 73. (d) 74. (d)

75. The work of 'finding out what is to be done and determine the best method of doing it' is known as
    (a) Job evaluation (b) Job Classification
    (c) Job description (d) Job Analysis
76. Zero-based budgeting was developed by
    (a) Peter Phyrr (b) Douglas McGregor
    (c) S.R Ranganathan (d) Elton Mayo
77. The standard height of a reading table is
    (a) 60cm (b) 75cm
    (c) 90cm (d) 100cm
78. One gigabyte is equal to
    (a) 1000 KB (b) 100000KB
    (c) 1000000KB (d) 10000000KB
79. Which of the following is not an output device?
    (a) Floppy disc (b) CD-ROM
    (c) Mouse (d) Printer
80. Which of the following is system software?
    (a) Windows (b) Open Office
    (c) Access (d) CDS/ISIS
81. In telecommunication, ISDN stands for
    (a) Integrated source digital network
    (b) International services digital network
    (c) International sources digital network
    (d) Integrated services digital network
82. Which one of the following is an internet browser?
    (a) Internet explorer (b) Google
    (c) Yahoo (d) Alta vista

Answer : 75. (d) 76. (a) 77. (b) 78. (c) 79. (c)
80. (a) 81. (d) 82. (a)

83. 'Gaseous treatment of material to destroy micro-organism and infestation by insects' is known as
(a) Encapsulation (b) Fumigation
(c) Oxidation (d) De-acidification

84. A standing vendor means
(a) A bookseller selected for supplying documents based on quotations
(b) A bookseller selected for supplying documents based on reputation for a fixed period of time
(c) A bookseller appointed permanently for the supply of documents
(d) A bookseller who supplies standing order books

85. Asia- Pacific international Network in Social Sciences (APINESS) is located at
(a) Manila (b) Bangok
(c) Singapore (d) New Delhi

86. A typical example of purely enumerative scheme of classification is
(a) Bibliographic classification
(b) Dewey Decimal Classification
(c) Library of Congress Classification
(d) Universal Decimal Classification

87. "A statement about which we cannot use either of the epithets right or wrong" is called
(a) Canon (b) Postulate
(c) Isolate (d) Theory

88. "A digit prefixed to an isolate number to indicate the fundamental category of which the isolate is a manifestation" is called as
(a) Indicator digit (b) Empty digit
(c) Emptying digit (d) Empty-emptying digit

Answer : 83. (b) 84. (b) 85. (b) 86. (c) 87. (b) 88. (a)

89. The number of the kinds of phase relations recognized in the latest edition of Colon Classification

    (a) 3 (b) 4
    (c) 5 (d) 6

90. "A catalogue in which all the entries are word entries" is called

    (a) Classified catalogue code
    (b) Printed catalogue
    (c) Card catalogue
    (d) Dictionary catalogue

91. The term "recall value" refers to

    (a) The quality of being called back to memory
    (b) The quality of retrieving more items
    (c) The quality of retrieving only relevant items
    (d) The quality of being identified easily

92. The technology that can be successfully used for digitalization of old books is

    (a) MICR technology (b) OMR technology
    (c) OCR technology (d) RFID technology

93. 'A catalogue listing in one sequence the holdings or part of the holdings of two or more libraries' is called

    (a) Co-operative catalogue
    (b) Centralised catalogue
    (c) Union catalogue
    (d) Shared catalogue

94. The principle of Osmosis can be applied in

    (a) Re-classification
    (b) Re-cataloguing
    (c) Retrospective conversion
    (d) In all the above

Answer : 89. (d) 90. (d) 91. (a) 92. (c) 93. (c) 94. (d)

95. Which one of the following is not an integrated library software ?
    (a) CDS/ISIS (b) Libsys
    (c) Alice for windows (d) SOUL
96. Which of the following is not a multimedia encyclopedia?
    (a) World book encyclopedia
    (b) Encarta
    (c) New Encyclopadia Britannica
    (d) Compton's interactive encyclopedia
97. Which of the following is an American Dictionary?
    (a) Oxford English Dictionary
    (b) Longman Dictionary of English Language
    (c) The Chambers dictionary
    (d) Webster's third new international dictionary
98. *Malayalam Grandhasoochi* is a publication
    (a) National library, Kolkatta
    (b) Kerala Sahitya academy
    (c) DC Books
    (d) Sahitya pravartaka co-operative society
99. *Sarva vijnana kosam is being published by*
    (a) Sahitya pravartaka co-operative society
    (b) DC Books
    (c) State Institute of languages
    (d) State institute of Encyclopedic publications
100. The binary code scheme that uses two bytes for each character providing 65539 possible characters known as
    (a) ASCI-8 (b) EBCDIC
    (c) Unicode (d) None of the above

Answer : 95. (a) 96. (c) 97. (d) 98. (b) 99. (d) 100. (c)

TEST OF LIBRARIAN Grade-3 FOR IHRD

By LBS Centre for Science and Technology

2009

1. The term *bibliometrics* was coined by
   (a) de Solla Prince (b) Alan Prichard
   (c) F.W Lancaster (d) B.C Brookes
2. Example of an Internet book shop is
   (a) Google.com (b) Yahoo.com
   (c) Amazone.com (d) Scirus.com
3. Demand theory of book selection was put forward by
   (a) Dewey (b) Drury
   (c) Mc Clovin (d) Ranganathan
4. The present edition of *New Encyclopaedia Britannica* consists of
   (a) One part and index
   (b) Two parts and index
   (c) Three parts and index
   (d) Four parts and index
5. International conference on cataloguing principle was held at
   (a) London (b) New York
   (c) Paris (d) Washington

Answer : 1. (b) 2. (c) 3. (c) 4. (d) 5. (c)

6. Census of India belongs to the category of
   (a) Biographical source
   (b) Year book
   (c) Statistical source
   (d) Current information source
7. Institute of Scientific Information (ISI) is located at
   (a) Philadelphia (b) Chicago
   (c) California (d) Rome
8. The periodicity of Indian National Bibliography is
   (a) Monthly (b) Weekly
   (c) Fortnightly (d) Annual
9. NISCAIR was formed by the amalgamation of
   (a) NISCOM and INSDOCC
   (b) INSDOC and NISTADS
   (c) NISCOM and NISTADS
   (d) INSDOC and NISSAT
10. Five laws of Library Science were formulated by Ranganathan in
   (a) 1940 (b) 1948
   (c) 1924 (d) 1931
11. *NUCSSI* stands for
   (a) National Union Catalogue of Scientific Serials in India
   (b) National Union Catalogue of Social Science Serials in India
   (c) National Union Catalogue of Science Serials in India
   (d) National Union Catalogue of Social Science & Science Serials in India

---

Answer : 6. (c) 7. (a) 8. (a) 9. (a) 10. (d) 11. (a)

12. The Theory of hierarchy of human needs was formulated by
   (a) Drucker (b) Herzberg
   (c) Maslow (d) Fayol
13. Henry Fayol, the famous management thinker was
   (a) French (b) Italian
   (c) American (d) German
14. In India, 'Librarians Day' is celebrated on
   (a) April 23 (b) Sept 24
   (c) Aug 12 (d) Nov 14
15. In a no-automated library, authority file is kept at
   (a) Acquisition section (b) Technical section
   (c) Maintenance section (d) Circulation section
16. National Science library was established at
   (a) NISSAT (b) DESIDOC
   (c) INSDOC (d) NASSDOC
17. The first national level library association is
   (a) American Library Association
   (b) Library Association
   (c) Indian Library Association
   (d) Canadian Library Association
18. Indian input centre of INIS database is
   (a) ICAR (b) BARC
   (c) TIFR (d) ISRO
19. Raja Rammohun Roy Library Foundation (RRLF) was established in connection with
   (a) Birth centenary of Raja Rammohun Roy
   (b) Second Birth centenary of Raja Rammohun Roy
   (c) Death centenary of Raja Rammohun Roy
   (d) None of these

Answer : 12. (c) 13. (c) 14. (c) 15. (a) 16. (c) 17. (a) 18. (b) 19. (a)

20. Who is the proponent of the concept 'global village'?
    (a) Daniel Bell (b) Alexander Grahmbell
    (c) Engine Garfield (d) Marshell McLuhan
21. Which of the following is not an operating system?
    (a) Linux (b) OS/2
    (c) Windows (d) Access
22. At present, ISBN has how many digits?
    (a) 8 (b) 12
    (c) 13 (d) 10
23. Which of the following is a Boolean logic operator?
    (a) ON (b) WITH
    (c) NOT (d) OF
24. Which of the following is not a yearly publication?
    (a) Statesman's Almanac
    (b) India: a reference annual
    (c) Books in Print
    (d) British National Bibliography
25. Web of knowledge is a product of
    (a) Thomson ISI (b) Elsevier
    (c) Wilson (d) R.R Bowker
26. The word incunabula stand for
    (a) Permission of the religious authority to publish a book
    (b) Earlier writing material
    (c) Books in the early stage of printing
    (d) A peculiar type of printing
27. The Alexandrian library was established by
    (a) Alexander the Great (b) Ptolemy
    (c) Callimachus (d) Julius Caesar

Answer : 20. (d) 21. (d) 22. (c) 23. (c) 24. (d) 25. (a) 26. (c) 27. (a)

28. When was the delivery of books and newspaper act passed in India?
    (a) 1954 (b) 1974
    (c) 1976 (d) 1990
29. The Classification Scheme used in *Indian Science Abstract* is
    (a) Dewey Decimal Classification
    (b) Universal Decimal Classification
    (c) Colon Classification
    (d) Library of Congress Classification
30. The name of e-journal consortium offered by INFLIBNET
    (a) NICNET (b) INDONET
    (c) JANET (d) INFONET
31. Delhi public library was established with the support of
    (a) IFLA (b) FID
    (c) UNESCO (d) British Library
32. The journal *Annals of library and Information Studies*
    (a) NISCAIR (b) NASSCOM
    (c) DESIDOC (d) IASLIC
33. The spiral of scientific method has
    (a) Two quadrants (b) Three quadrants
    (c) Four quadrants (d) Five quadrants
34. The expansion of DELNET
    (a) Delhi library Network
    (b) Digital library Network
    (c) Delegated library Network
    (d) Distant library Network

Answer : 28. (a) 29. (a) 30. (d) 31. (c) 32. (d) 33. (c) 34. (a)

35. Which of the following is not input device?
    (a) Monitor (b) Joystick
    (c) CD-ROM (d) Modem
36. Which is the first library science journal?
    (a) Libri
    (b) Library journal
    (c) Journal of documentation
    (d) Library literature
37. *Science Citation Index* was started in
    (a) 1984 (b) 1974
    (c) 1964 (d) 1994
38. Which University started the MLISc course for the first time among the commonwealth countries?
    (a) Banaras Hindu University
    (b) Aligarh Muslim University
    (c) Delhi University
    (d) Madras University
39. The book number system devised by S.R Ranganathan is based on
    (a) Subject (b) Year of publication
    (c) Name of author (d) Title of the book
40. The term used by Ranganathan for reservation of book is
    (a) Bespeaking (b) Booking
    (c) Advancing (d) Prioritizing
41. The secondary education commission, 1953 is known as
    (a) Radhakrishna commission
    (b) Mudaliyar commission
    (c) Kothari commission
    (d) Ranganathan commission

Answer : 35. (d) 36. (a) 37. (c) 38. (c) 39. (c) 40. (a) 41. (b)

42. The expansion of ERNET is
    (a) Entertainment Resource Network
    (b) Educational Resource Network
    (c) Experimental Research Network
    (d) Education and Research Network
43. Government publications are generally treated as
    (a) Primary sources
    (b) Secondary sources
    (c) Tertiary sources
    (d) Ready reference source
44. The term 'grey literature' refers to
    (a) Publication not available through normal channels
    (b) Publication with grey cover
    (c) Literature dealing with old people
    (d) Literature which do not have lasting value
45. The work concerned with keeping of books on shelves in the correct order is known as
    (a) Stock verification (b) Shelf study
    (c) Shelf rectification (d) Shelf relocation
46. According to Dewey Decimal Classification, the main subject of the title *treatment of vetinary diseases is*
    (a) Agriculture (b) Zoology
    (c) Medicine (d) None of these
47. Cover to cover translation is an example of
    (a) On demand service
    (b) Anticipatory service
    (c) Information consolidation
    (d) Reprographic service

Answer : 42. (d) 43. (a) 44. (a) 45. (c) 46. (c) 47. (a)

48. A meta-search engine is a?
    (a) Most used search engine
    (b) One which searches in more than one search engines at the same line
    (c) One which can be contacted only through other search engines
    (d) One which gives precise results
49. The most used information sources in Science and Technology are
    (a) Journals (b) Research reports
    (c) Standards (d) Theses
50. The address of a web resource is referred to as
    (a) HTML (b) HTTP
    (c) URL (d) WWW
51. In the context of library classification, the property of notation that acts as an aid to memory is known as
    (a) Expressiveness (b) Mnemonics
    (c) Brevity (d) Hospitality
52. Which of the following is an example of a relational database management system?
    (a) Ms-Word (b) Ms-Excel
    (c) Lotus 1-2-3 (d) Oracle
53. Paris principles deals with
    (a) Objectives of a library catalogue
    (b) Metadata standards
    (c) Standards for bibliographic description
    (d) Networking topologies

Answer : 48. (b) 49. (b) 50. (c) 51. (b) 52. (d) 53. (c)

54. The *Bibliographic Classification was devised by*
    (a) S.R Ranganathan (b) H.E Bliss
    (c) Rider (d) J D Brown
55. The creator of World Wide Web?
    (a) Jack Kilby (b) Sabir Bhatia
    (c) Richard Stallman (d) Tim Berness-Lee
56. The *Sears list of subject heading* was originally devised by
    (a) Reubuck Sears
    (b) Rachl Susanne Sears
    (c) Minnie Earl Sears
    (d) Edward Brennan Sears
57. *UNIMAC* was brought out in 1977 by
    (a) IFLA (b) FID
    (c) ISO (d) BSI
58. The abbreviation for World Wide Web consortium is?
    (a) W3C (b) WC3
    (c) 3WC (d) 3WC3
59. AACR2 allows up to ....areas in each catalogue entry
    (a) 5 (b) 6
    (c) 7 (d) 8
60. The 'Wealth of India' is the publication of
    (a) ICAR
    (b) CSIR
    (c) ICMR
    (d) Publication Division, Govt. of India

Answer : 54. (b) 55. (d) 56. (c) 57. (a) 58. (a)
59. (b) 60. (d)

61. The abbreviation of TCP/IP is
    (a) Transmission control protocol /Internet protocol
    (b) Transmission of control protocol/Internet protocol
    (c) Transmission control of protocol/Internet protocol
    (d) Transmission of control protocols/ Internet protocols

62. The library management software developed by INFLIBNET is
    (a) E-Granthalaya (b) Alice for windows
    (c) Libsys (d) SOUL

63. Unicode, a superset of ASCII, uses a ....bit of code for each character
    (a) 7 (b) 8
    (c) 16 (d) 64

64. 'Which of the following was not a network operating system?
    (a) Novell Netware (b) Macintosh
    (c) Unix (d) Windows NT

65. Examples of broadband communication channel is
    (a) Ultra violet rays (b) Twisted pair cable
    (c) Optical fiber cable (d) Infrared rays

66. The publisher of *Ulrich's periodical directory* is
    (a) Whittaker (b) Bowker
    (c) Elsevier (d) Wilson

Answer : 61. (a) 62. (d) 63. (b) 64. (c) 65. (b) 66. (d)

67. The information facility at the national level established by UGC for the benefit of teachers and research scholars is
    (a) ERNET (b) NICNET
    (c) NCSI (d) RENNIC
68. A source which contains the lines of Indian National Anthem is
    (a) India: a reference annual
    (b) Gazetteer of India
    (c) Encyclopedia Britannica
    (d) Encyclopedia Americana
69. Which of the following committee is not seen in libraries?
    (a) Executive committee
    (b) Advisory committee
    (c) Book selection committee
    (d) Appointment committee
70. A commonly used method in libraries to avoid the attack of biological pests is
    (a) Fumigation (b) Sterilization
    (c) Lamination (d) Mounting
71. *Three card system* devised by Ranganathan consists of
    (a) Register card, top card and bottom card
    (b) Register card, check card, and top card
    (c) Register card, check card and top card
    (d) Register card, check card and classified index card

Answer : 67. (a) 68. (a) 69. (d) 70. (a) 71. (d)

72. PRECIS is an example of
   (a) Pre-coordinate indexing system
   (b) Post coordinate indexing system
   (c) Nested phase indexing system
   (d) Free text indexing system

73. Normally, registration of members is carried out by
   (a) Acquisition section (b) Technical section
   (c) Reference section (d) Circulation section

74. The process of welcoming new staff members and introducing them to the library and explaining the activities to be carried out is called
   (a) Training
   (b) Personnel specification
   (c) Initiation of fresh man
   (d) Introduction

75. National Social Science Documentation Centre (NASSDO(C) is a part of
   (a) CSIR (b) ICHR
   (c) ICSSR (d) ICCR

76. Which one of the five laws emphasizes the need of library legislation?
   (a) 1st (b) 2nd
   (c) 3rd (d) 4th

77. The chief source of information for cataloguing a book is
   (a) Cover page (b) Title leaf
   (c) Overflow pages (d) Preface

Answer : 72. (a) 73. (d) 74. (a) 75. (c) 76. (b) 77. (b)

78. Which of the following record reflects the arrangements of documents in the shelves?

(a) Shelf list (b) Accession register
(c) Authority file (d) Order file

79. The British libraries in India are controlled jointly by................British Council

(a) India international centre
(b) Indian Council for Cultural relations
(c) Ministry of foreign affairs
(d) RRLF

80. The entries in *Commonwealth universities handbook* are arranged

(a) In the alphabetical order of countries
(b) In the alphabetical order of universities
(c) In the chronological order of universities
(d) None of the above

81. Which of the following is not library management software?

(a) Granthalya (b) Libsys
(c) Libsuite (d) CDS/ISIS

82. *Psychological abstract* is brought out by

(a) American psychological association
(b) British psychology society
(c) Commonwealth association of psychologists
(d) Canadian psychological association

83. The earliest encyclopedia in Malayalam is

(a) Sarvavijnankosam (b) Viswavijnanakosam
(c) Akhilvijnankosam (d) Vijnanam

Answer : 78. (a) 79. (d) 80. (b) 81. (a) 82. (a) 83. (a)

84. *Malayala Grandha soochi,* the comprehensive bibliography of books in Malayalam is a project of
    (a) University of Kerala
    (b) Kerala sahitya academy
    (c) Department of Culture
    (d) National library, Calcutta
85. Malayalam lexicon is being published by
    (a) Kerala sahitya academy
    (b) D.C Books
    (c) University of Kerala
    (d) State Institute of languages
86. A Malayalam encyclopedia available in CD format is
    (a) Vijnanam (b) Sarvavijnanakosam
    (c) Viswavijnanakosam (d) Akhilavijnanakosam
87. Which university established the first school of Library Science?
    (a) Cornel (b) Columbia
    (c) London (d) Yale
88. Association of college and Research libraries (ACRL) is a part of
    (a) American Library Association
    (b) Library Association
    (c) Canadian library Association
    (d) Australian Library Association
89. The proponent of zero based budgeting is
    (a) Henri Fayol (b) Peter Phyrr
    (c) Chester Bernard (d) S.R Ranganathan

Answer : 84. (b) 85. (d) 86. (c) 87. (b) 88. (c) 89. (b)

90. NPAC is a programme concerned with
    (a) Shared cataloguing (b) Shared storage
    (c) Shared classification (d) Sharing of computers
91. In chain procedure, there can be sought link, unsought link and...
    (a) Subject link (b) Heading link
    (c) Phase link (d) False link
92. The only code in the English language meant for a classified catalogue is
    (a) CCC (b) AARC I
    (c) ALA Code (d) AACR II
93. When was Indian copyright act was passed
    (a) 1954 (b) 1970
    (c) 1994 (d) 1957
94. The compiler of famous publication 'A world Bibliography of Bibliographies' is
    (a) Walford (b) Besterman
    (c) Winchel (d) Webster
95. As per the staff formula recommended by Ranganathan, in the Technical section one professional can do the technical processing of how many books?
    (a) 5000- 6000 (b) 3000- 4000
    (c) 2000- 2500 (d) 1500- 2000
96. Guides to Literature in different subjects belong to the category of
    (a) Primary sources
    (b) Secondary sources
    (c) Tertiary sources
    (d) Ready reference source

Answer : 90. (a) 91. (d) 92. (b) 93. (d) 94. (b) 95. (d) 96. (c)

97. The size of a catalogue card is
(a) 3.5 x 5.5 cm (b) 7 x 12cm
(c) 5 x 8cm (d) 7.5 x 12.5cm

98. A catalogue tray can contain approximately .... Catalogue cards
(a) 700 (b) 1000
(c) 1500 (d) 1250

99. Display guides used in the stack room include
(a) Tier guide, gangway guide, bay guide, shelf guide
(b) Tier guide, roof guide, bay guide, shelf guide
(c) Tier guide, gangway guide, wall guide, shelf guide
(d) Tier guide, gangway guide, bay guide, step guide

100. According to Kothari Commission, a university should provide .... Percent of the budget to its library?
(a) 20 (b) 5-7
(c) 6 (d) 6.5-10

Answer : 97. (d) 98. (b) 99. (a) 100. (d)

PUBLIC SERVICE COMMISSION-KERALA

Examination for Librarian Grade-4

January 2008

1. The term Bibliometrics was first used by
   (a) Allen Kent (b) S.R Ranganathan
   (c) S.C Bradford (d) Allan Pritchard
2. SANJAY software for libraries is devised by
   (a) INSDOC (b) NASSDOC
   (c) UNESCO (d) DESIDOC
3. Scientific method of Research can be used
   (a) Humanities (b) Social Science
   (c) Applied Science (d) All disciplines
4. The acronym of Association for Information Management is
   (a) IMA (b) AIM
   (c) ASLIB (d) MIA
5. RRLF Kolkatta provides financial support to what type of libraries?
   (a) Academic (b) Special
   (c) Public (d) National
6. The book 'Rules for a dictionary catalogue' was written by
   (a) James Duff Brown (b) C.A Cutter
   (c) Allen Kent (d) S.R Ranganathan

Answer : 1. (d) 2. (d) 3. (d) 4. (c) 5. (c) 6. (b)

7. The three connectors AND, OR and NOT used in search statements are know as
   (a) Logical sum (b) SDI
   (c) Venn Diagram (d) Boolean operators
8. Good Offices Committee (GO(C) was constituted in
   (a) 1980 (b) 1971
   (c) 1985 (d) 1975
9. The name of INSDOC is changed to
   (a) NISCAIR (b) NASSDOC
   (c) NISH (d) INIS
10. International conference of cataloguing principles, 1961 was held in
    (a) London (b) New York
    (c) Paris (d) Copenhagen
11. Information services for physics and engineering communities are called
    (a) Physics Abstracts (b) MEDLARS
    (c) Engineering Index (d) INSPEC
12. Asian Recorder is published
    (a) Monthly (b) Fortnightly
    (c) Weekly (d) Bi weekly
13. 'Laws of Scattering' which forms the foundation of bibliometrics is described by
    (a) A.J Lotka (b) G.K Zipf
    (c) S.C Bradford (d) E.Garfield
14. Who coined the term 'information retrieval'?
    (a) F.W Lancaster (b) Faradane
    (c) Calvin Moores (d) S.R Ranganathan

Answer : 7. (d) 8. (b) 9. (a) 10. (c) 11. (d) 12. (c) 13. (c) 14. (c)

15. The first book authored by S.R Ranganathan is
    (a) Library manual
    (b) Colon classification
    (c) Five laws of library science
    (d) Documentation
16. British National Bibliography (BN(B) is a
    (a) Primary source of information
    (b) Secondary source of information
    (c) Tertiary source of information
    (d) None of the above
17. The first director of DRTC was
    (a) S.R Ranganathan (b) P.N Kaula
    (c) B.S Kesavan (d) I.K Ravichandra Rao
18. The CDS/ISIS software was developed by
    (a) NISSAT (b) INSDOC
    (c) DRTC (d) UNESCO
19. The term used to define physical devices of a computer is
    (a) Monitor (b) Software
    (c) Hardware (d) CPU
20. "India: a reference annual" is an example of
    (a) Hand book (b) Year book
    (c) Statistical source (d) Directory
21. Which law of library science emphasized library legislation?
    (a) First law (b) Second law
    (c) Third law (d) Fourth law

Answer : 15. (c) 16. (b) 17. (a) 18. (d) 19. (c) 20. (b) 21. (b)

22. "Asian recorder" is published from
    (a) Kolkatta (b) Peeking
    (c) Colombo (d) New Delhi
23. The headquarters of IFLA is at
    (a) Paris (b) London
    (c) The Hague (d) New York
24. Indian Science Abstract is published by
    (a) CSIR (b) IASLIC
    (c) NISCAIR (d) DESIDOC
25. Which term was coined by Ranganathan for mobile library?
    (a) Library on wheels (b) Librarchine
    (c) Moving library (d) None of these
26. Gazetteers are popularly known as
    (a) Handbook of maps
    (b) Statistical atlas
    (c) Directory of place names
    (d) A geographical dictionary
27. 'Grey literature' means
    (a) Archival documents
    (b) Audio-visual material
    (c) Unpublished documents
    (d) Classified documents
28. The library Association (UK) was founded in
    (a) 1875 (b) 1876
    (c) 1877 (d) 1870

Answer : 22. (d) 23. (c) 24. (c) 25. (b) 26. (d) 27. (c) 28. (c)

29. Which of the following information about India is available in "wealth of India"?
    (a) Industry and commerce
    (b) Technology, computers
    (c) Society, economic development
    (d) Raw materials and industrial products
30. FID was founded by
    (a) Sayers and Batty
    (b) Paul Otlet and Henry La fontain
    (c) Garfield and Lancaster
    (d) Ranganathan and Bhattacharya
31. Libraries are considered as repositories of
    (a) Audio-visual
    (b) Religious books
    (c) Information and knowledge
    (d) Furniture and equipment
32. "Current Contents" published by Institute of Scientific information is an example of what kind of service?
    (a) Reference (b) Abstracting
    (c) Current awareness (d) News paper clipping
33. Ranganathan's five laws of library science are a set of norms of
    (a) Information service (b) Information system
    (c) Librarianship (d) Documentation
34. Document delivery service is an example of
    (a) Anticipatory service
    (b) Reference service
    (c) Current awareness service
    (d) On demand service

Answer : 29. (d) 30. (b) 31. (c) 32. (b) 33. (c) 34. (d)

35. Information and Library Network (INFLIBNET)

(a) NBT (b) RRLF

(c) UGC (d) NISSAT

36. When data is processed, interpreted and presented in an organized logical form, it becomes

(a) Knowledge (b) Intelligence

(c) Facts (d) Information

37. Which public libraries act provides an independent minister for Library Service?

(a) Manipur (b) Kerala

(c) Mizoram (d) West Bengal

38. Yearbook and manuals are which type of sources?

(a) Bibliographic (b) Primary

(c) Ready reference (d) Tertiary

39. Standard size of card catalogue is

(a) 5.5 x 8.5cm (b) 10.5 x 7.5 cm

(c) 7.5 x 12.5cm (d) 6.5 x 11.5cm

40. Right information to the right user is the implication of which law of library science?

(a) First (b) Second

(c) Third (d) Fourth

41. There are two charging systems quite popular in Indian libraries, one Browne charging system and the other is

(a) Dewey charging system

(b) Newark charging system

(c) Mills charging system

(d) Ranganathan charging system

Answer : 35. (c) 36. (a) 37. (d) 38. (c) 39. (c) 40. (c) 41. (b)

42. Librarian of Library of Congress is appointed by
    (a) Chairman, Congress
    (b) President of Library of Congress
    (c) President of USA
    (d) Chief executive, Library affairs
43. Which is the oldest form of library co-operation?
    (a) Internet (b) Library automation
    (c) Inter-library loan (d) Library network
44. Public library acts enables to create a cadre of
    (a) Indian information
    (b) All India library service
    (c) State library service
    (d) Subordinate library
45. Which act provides reservation of one woman and one ST member to all library committees?
    (a) Goa (b) Kerala
    (c) Gujarat (d) Manipur
46. A record of all traditional entries is known as
    (a) Book index entry (b) Added entry
    (c) Tracing (d) Unit card
47. Which is the state library of Tamilnadu?
    (a) Madres University library
    (b) Ranganathan institute of library studies
    (c) Oriental library
    (d) Cannemara public library
48. Entries that go into a catalogue for parts and chapters of a book is known as
    (a) Chapter entries (b) Main entries
    (c) Analytical entries (d) Reference entries

Answer : 42. (c) 43. (c) 44. (c) 45. (b) 46. (c) 47. (d) 48. (c)

49. IFLA has developed an internationally acceptable bibliographic standard namely

(a) UK-MARC (b) CCF

(c) US-MARC (d) UNIMARC

50. In CCC, the editor of series entry is called

(a) Book index entry

(b) Cross reference entry

(c) Class index entry

(d) Cross reference index entry

51. The president of the Kerala state library council is

(a) George Onakoor

(b) Balamohan thampy

(c) Kadammanitta Ramakrishnan

(d) M.A Baby

52. The journal 'Annals of Library and Information studies' is published by

(a) IASLIC (b) ILA

(c) NISCAIR (d) DESIDOC

53. CCF stands for

(a) Current Communication Format

(b) Common Classification Format

(c) Common Communication Format

(d) Current Classification Format

54. 'Unit is strength' is the principle of management advocated by

(a) Taylor (b) Bernard

(c) Fayol (d) S.R Ranganathan

Answer : 49. (d) 50. (a) 51. (b) 52. (c) 53. (c) 54. (d)

55. The internationally agreed upon number given to a book is known as
    (a) ISSN (b) ISDN
    (c) ISBN (d) ISMN
56. Bureau of Indian Standards (BIS) is located at
    (a) New Delhi (b) Mumbai
    (c) Kolkata (d) Dehradun
57. MEDLARS is designed by
    (a) Medical library association
    (b) National medical library
    (c) National library of medicine
    (d) Medical council
58. 'Indian books in print' is an example of which bibliography
    (a) Trade (b) National
    (c) Universal (d) Subject
59. Motivating the potential users to use information resource is known as
    (a) Users profile
    (b) User orientation
    (c) Bibliographic instruction
    (d) User education
60. 'Grandhalokam' is published by
    (a) The Kerala sastra sahitya parisat
    (b) Kerala state library council
    (c) National library
    (d) Kerala sahitya academy

Answer : 55. (c) 56. (c) 57. (a) 58. (a) 59. (d) 60. (b)

61. The earlier name of national library, Kolkata was
    (a) National information centre
    (b) National public library
    (c) Calcutta public library
    (d) The imperial library
62. Kerala enacted public libraries Act in the year
    (a) 1958 (b) 1989
    (c) 1990 (d) 1887
63. Indian Library Association (IL(A) was founded in the year
    (a) 1933 (b) 1935
    (c) 1925 (d) 1946
64. The prolegomena to Library Classification was written by
    (a) M.A Gopinath (b) P.N Kaula
    (c) K.A Isaac (d) S.R Ranganathan
65. India: a reference annual is
    (a) serial (b) Periodical
    (c) Quarterly (d) Monthly
66. Encyclopedia of Library Science is edited by
    (a) S.R Ranganathan (b) Melvil Dewey
    (c) A.C Foskette (d) Allen Kent
67. A thing or an idea is called
    (a) Universe (b) Entity
    (c) Group (d) Class
68. Who defined classification as, "the arrangement of books on shelves or description of them in the manner which is most helpful to those who read?
    (a) H.E Bliss (b) T.D Brown
    (c) S.R Ranganathan (d) W.C.B Sayers

Answer : 61. (d) 62. (b) 63. (a) 64. (d) 65. (a) 66. (d) 67. (b) 68. (d)

69. UDC is an extended version of
    (a) CC (b) DDC
    (c) CCF (d) LC
70. Class number denotes
    (a) Year of publication (b) AUTHOR
    (c) Editor (d) Specific subject
71. Astrophysics and Biochemistry are example of
    (a) Loose assemblage (b) Distillation
    (c) Agglomeration (d) Fusion
72. The recurring concept in Colon Classification are called
    (a) Auxiliary (b) Standard Subdivision
    (c) Special auxiliaries (d) Common auxiliaries
73. A digit with an ordinal value but without a semantic value is called
    (a) Empty digit (b) Empty-emptying digit
    (c) Emptying digit (d) Special digit
74. The connecting symbol for time in UD C is
    (a) Dot
    (b) Plus
    (c) Double Inverted commas
    (d) Semicolon
75. List of documents in a library is called
    (a) Bibliography (b) Union catalogue
    (c) Latest edition (d) Library catalogue
76. Chemical abstract is published
    (a) Fortnightly (b) Yearly
    (c) Monthly (d) Weekly

Answer : 69. (b) 70. (d) 71. (d) 72. (d) 73. (a) 74. (c) 75. (d) 76. (d)

77. Keesings record of world events is an example of
    (a) Newspaper index (b) News digests
    (c) News letter (d) News archive
78. UGC centre for science information is located at
    (a) New Delhi (b) Hyderabad
    (c) Trivandrum (d) Bangalore
79. Compendex is the online database on
    (a) Chemistry (b) Geology
    (c) Physics (d) Engineering
80. Database is a collection of
    (a) Records (b) Information
    (c) Bytes (d) Files.
81. OPAC stands for
    (a) Online preparation of cataloguing
    (b) Online Public Access Catalogue
    (c) Operating Automated Catalogue
    (d) Ohio Public Access Catalogue
82. Software may be defined as
    (a) A set of files (b) A set of programs
    (c) A set of packages (d) A Set of databases
83. FDT stands for
    (a) Format design table (b) Format deletion table
    (c) Field definition table (d) Field design table
84. When is the national Library Week of India Celebrated?
    (a) 14-20th November (b) 1-6 November
    (c) 1-6th November (d) None of the above

Answer : 77. (d) 78. (d) 79. (d) 80. (a) 81. (b)
82. (b) 83. (c) 84. (a)

85. Who is the father of library science in India?
    (a) B.S Kesavan (b) P.N Panikar
    (c) S.Bashirudheen (d) S.R Ranganathan
86. What is the class number of Malayalam Poetry according to 7th edition of CC?
    (a) O.32,1 (b) O,32,1
    (c) O,321 (d) O.321
87. Who said the following words?
    "The extent of use to which the reading material of a library is put, should determine its importance rather than the staggering number of volumes".
    (a) Plato (b) Fracis Bacon
    (c) Tagore (d) S.R Ranganathan
88. Who edited Sayers Manual of Classification for librarians, Ed5, 1975?
    (a) P.N Kaula (b) H.E Bliss
    (c) S.R Ranganathan (d) Arthur Maltby
89. Name the author of the book "Towards paperless Information systems"
    (a) S.R Ranganathan (b) J.D Brown
    (c) F.W Lancaster (d) J.H Shera
90. Who devised the motto of the ALA "The best reading for the largest number at the least cost"?
    (a) Melvil Dewey (b) H.E Bliss
    (c) Lionel R.Mc Colvin (d) P.N Kaula
91. The notation of CC is
    (a) Pure (b) Mixed
    (c) Decimal (d) Semantic

Answer : 85. (d) 86. (b) 87. (c) 88. (d) 89. (c) 90. (a) 91. (b)

92. The major function of circulation section of a library is
    (a) Book ordering
    (b) Cataloguing
    (c) Issue and return of books
    (d) Reference service
93. One of the principles of facet sequence is
    (a) Later in evolution (b) Wall-picture
    (c) Later in time (d) Literary warrant
94. An array of classes consists of
    (a) Subordinate classes
    (b) Super ordinate classes
    (c) Co ordinate classes
    (d) Collateral classes
95. 'Hierarchy in subject is the only principle adopted in mapping of subjects in
    (a) CC (b) DDC
    (c) UDC (d) LC
96. According to AAR-II physical description about a document in a catalogue entry is called
    (a) Collation
    (b) Imprint
    (c) Physical description
    (d) Additional useful information
97. Ranganathan's chain procedure is based on
    (a) Canons of classification
    (b) Postulation approach
    (c) Calls number
    (d) Principle of facet sequence

Answer : 92. (c) 93. (b) 94. (c) 95. (b) 96. (a) 97. (c)

98. Staff formulae for University and College libraries in India
    (a) M.A Gopinath
    (b) S.R Ranganathan
    (c) C.D Deshmugh
    (d) Prof. Yashpal
99. Zip's law relates to
    (a) Core literature
    (b) Productivity of scientists
    (c) Word frequency ranking
    (d) Scattering of literature
100. In CCC the subject analytical entry is called
    (a) Cross reference index entry
    (b) Explanatory reference entry
    (c) Cross reference entry
    (d) Specific subject entry

Answer : 98. (b) 99. (c) 100. (a)

UGC –NATIONAL ELIGIBILITY TEST

Library & Information Science

JUNE 2010

1. Who expressed knowledge in a simple mathematical equation $k(s) + \Delta = k(s + \Delta s)$?
   (A) Eritz Machlup (B) B.C Brooks
   (C) N.J Belkin (D) C.E Shanon
2. Which is not near synonym term to information?
   (A) Ideas (B) Data
   (C) Catalogue (D) Facts
3. CCF stands for
   (A) Common Communication Format
   (B) Centre for Communication Format
   (C) Committee for Communication Format
   (D) Common Curriculum Format
4. Resource sharing among libraries was prompted by the factors
   (A) Price acceleration (B) Information explosion
   (C) Both A and B (D) None of the above
5. The library Association (UK) is now the component of
   (A) ASLIB (B) CILIP
   (C) ALA (D) None of the above

Answer : 1. (b) 2. (c) 3. (a) 4. (c) 5. (b)

6. Real time access refers to
   (A) Access in advance
   (B) Access after some time
   (C) Access when searched for
   (D) None of the above
7. Which of the following professional Association does not exist now?
   (A) IFLA (B) ALA
   (C) FID (D) IASLIC
8. Theory X and Theory Y relate to
   (A) Planning (B) Motivation
   (C) Innovation (D) None of the above
9. Dewey Decimal Classification is now looked after by
   (A) Lake Placid Club
   (B) Library of Congress
   (C) OCLC
   (D) Classification Research Group
10. INSDOC has been merged with
    (A) DELNET (B) NISCAIR
    (C) DESIDOC (D) NASSDOC
11. World Wide Web first designed by
    (A) Charles Babbage (B) F.W Taylor
    (C) Ted Nelson (D) Tim Berne's Lee
12. ISBN consists of
    (A) 6 digit (B) 8 digit
    (C) 13 digit (D) 15 digit

Answer : 6. (b) 7. (d) 8. (b) 9. (c) 10. (b) 11. (d) 12. (c)

13. Bibliographical coupling is related to
    (A) Bibliometric studies
    (B) Bibliography compilation
    (C) Modes of subject formation
    (D) Vocabulary control
14. Dublin Core metadata consists of
    (A) 15 elements (B) 10 elements
    (C) 25 elements (D) 08 elements
15. A type of indexing where terms are coordinated prior to searching
    (A) Post coordinate indexing
    (B) Pre coordinate indexing
    (C) Uniterm indexing
    (D) None of the above
16. Use of ICs were made in
    (A) First generation computers
    (B) Second generation computer
    (C) Third generation computers
    (D) Fourth generation computers
17. The network topology in which nodes are connected to a central hub is known as
    (A) Ring topology (B) Bus topology
    (C) Star topology (D) Mesh topology
18. Which of the following is a term used for working assumption of a solution to a problem?
    (A) Research (B) Hypothesis
    (C) Bibliography (D) Thesis
19. Computer memory measured in
    (A) Bytes (B) Kilobytes
    (C) Megabytes (D) All the above

Answer : 13. (a) 14. (a) 15. (a) 16. (c) 17. (c) 18. (b) 19. (d)

20. DELNET stands for

(A) Developing Library Network

(B) Department of Electronic Library Network

(C) Distance Education Library Network

(D) Delhi Library Network

21. Assertion ((A) : Demand is the only governing factor in Book selection

Reason (R) : Patron's requirements govern building library collection Codes:

(A) A is true and R is false

(B) A is false and R is true

(C) A and R both are true

(D) A and R both are false

22. Assertion ((A): An indexing language is much more than a list of index terms those are acceptable to users

Reason (R) : An indexing language helps users discriminate between terms and reduces ambiguity in the language.

Codes:

(A) Both A and R are true and R is not the correct explanation

(B) Both A and R are true and R is the correct explanation

(C) A is false but R is true

(D) A is true but R is false

Answer : 20. (d) 21. (b) 22. (b)

23. Assertion ((A) : Libraries are facing a threat and are bound to disappear soon

Reason (R) : Internet and WWW provides access to oceans of information worldwide.

Codes:

(A) A is true but R is false

(B) A is false but R is true

(C) A and R both are true

(D) A and R both are false

24. Assertion ((A): De acidification is a measure to preserve documents in any medium

Reason (R) : Digital preservation needs a different preservation care.

Codes:

(A) A is false but R is true

(B) A is true but R is false

(C) A and R both are true

(D) A and R both are false

25. Assertion (A) : SDI is a user oriented current information service

Reason (R) : It is an altering service directed towards groups

Codes:

(A) Both A and R are true

(B) A is true but R is false

(C) A is false but R is true

(D) Both A and R are false

Answer : 23. (b) 24. (a) 25. (b)

26. Assertion (A) : Indexing periodical retrieves information. Which includes brief summary of the article.

    Reason (R) : It provides list of articles along with the title, authors and other bibliographic details.

    Codes:

    (A) Both A and R are true
    (B) Both A and R are false
    (C) A is true but R is false
    (D) A is false but R is true

27. Assertion ((A) : Median is simply the middle value when the datahave been arranging in ascending or descending order.

    Reason (R) : Median refers to the middle value in a distribution.

    Codes:

    (A) Both A and R are true
    (B) A is true but R is false
    (C) A is false but R is true
    (D) Both A and R are false

28. Assertion (A): Data base is a collection of interrelated data stored together

    Reason (R) : It is an organized integrated collection of data

    Codes:

    (A) Both A and R are true
    (B) A is true but R is false
    (C) A is false but R is true
    (D) Both A and R are false

Answer : 26. (d) 27. (a) 28. (c)

29. Assertion (A) : Dewey Decimal is an enumerative scheme of classification

Reason (R) : The scheme has developed several devices and is no more an enumerative scheme of classification.

Codes:

(A) Both A and R are true

(B) A is true but R is false

(C) A is false but R is true

(D) Both A and R are false

30. Assertion (A): Library legislation provides proper governance and management.

Reason (R) : It ensures free public library service to all irrespective of caste, creed and sex.

Codes:

(A) Both A and R are true

(B) A is true but R is false

(C) A is false but R is true

(D) Both A and R are false

31. Arrange the following in the chronological sequence of their development

1) ISBD 2) CCF

3) FRBR 4) MARC

(A) 1,2,4,3 (B) 4,1,2,3

(C) 3,2,4,1 (D) 1,4,2,3

Answer : 29. (a) 30. (d) 31. (b)

32. Arrange the following secondary publication according to the beginning of their publication in chronological order.

1) Biological abstract	2) Chemical abstract
3) LISA	4) Index Medicus
(A) 1,2,4,3	(B) 4,1,2,3
(C) 3,2,4,1	(D) 1,4,2,3

33. Arrange the following state chronologically, according to year of enactment of Library Legislation

1) Tamilnadu	2) UP
3) Gujarat	4) Mizoram
(A) 4,3,1,2	(B) 2,4,3,1
(C) 1,4,3,2	(D) 1,2,4,3

34. Arrange the following chronologically according to their use in computers

1) Vacuum tube	2) Microchip
3) Integrated circuits	4) Transistors
(A) 1,3,2,4	(B) 1,2,3,4
(C) 1,4,3,2	(D) 2,4,3,1

35. Arrange the following professional associations according to the year of their establishment.

1) ILA	2) IASLIC
3) ALA	4) ASLIB
(A) 1,2,3,4	(B) 3,4,1,2
(C) 4,3,2,1	(D) 1,3,2,4

Answer : 32. (c) 33. (c) 34. (c) 35. (b)

36. Arrange the following according to their chronological order
    1) Universal copyright conservation
    2) Berne Convention
    3) Indian copyright act
    4) WIPO copyright act
    (A) 2,4,3,1 (B) 3,2,4,1
    (C) 1,3,2,4 (D) 2,1,3,4

37. Arrange structure of the research report in correct order
    1) Table of contents 2) Appendices
    3) Text 4) Title page
    (A) 3,1,4,2 (B) 1,2,3,4
    (C) 2,3,4,1 (D) 4,1,3,2

38. Arrange the following scheme of classification according to their year of publication
    1) CC 2) DDC
    3) LC 4) UDC
    (A) 2,1,3,4 (B) 2,3,4,1
    (C) 1,2,4,3 (D) 4,3,2,1

39. Match the following

	List -1	**List-2**
(a)	Right to Information act	1) 2000
(b)	Universal declaration of of human rights	2) 2005
(c)	IT Act	3) 1948
(d)	Digital Millennium Act	4) 1998

Codes:

	a	b	c	d
(A)	1	2	3	4
(B)	2	3	1	4
(C)	3	2	4	1
(D)	4	3	2	1

Answer : 36. (d) 37. (d) 38. (b) 39. (b)

40. Match the following

	List -1	**List-2**
(a)	Father of scientific management	1) Henry Fayaol
(b)	Father of administration	2) Elton Mayo
(c)	Father of Human relation school	3) F. Herzberg
(d)	Father of corporate strategy	4) F.W Taylor

Codes:

	a	b	c	d
(A)	4	2	1	3
(B)	4	1	2	3
(C)	3	4	2	1
(D)	2	3	4	1

41. Match the following

	List -1	**List-2**
(a)	C.A Cutter	1) Bibliographic classification
(b)	H.E Bliss	2) Expansive classification
(c)	J.D Brown	3) Universal classification
(d)	Paul Otlet & Henry La Fontain	4) Subject classification

Codes:

	a	b	c	d
(A)	2	1	4	3
(B)	2	3	4	1
(C)	1	3	4	2
(D)	3	4	2	1

Answer : 40. (b) 41. (a)

42. Match the following

List -1	List-2
(a) International conference on Cataloguing principles	1) 1969
(b) International meeting of Cataloguing experts	2) 1961
(c) International symposium of Bibliographic exchange	3) 1990
(d) First CCF users meeting	4) 1978

Codes:

	a	b	c	d
(A)	2	1	4	3
(B)	3	2	4	1
(C)	4	3	1	2
(D)	3	1	4	2

43. Match the following

List -1	List-2
(a) NASSDOC	1) Defence science
(b) DEVSIS	2) Social sciences
(c) INIS	3) Development science
(d) DESIDOC	4) Nuclear science

Codes:

	a	b	c	d
(A)	4	2	1	3
(B)	2	3	4	1
(C)	1	2	3	4
(D)	3	2	1	4

Answer : 42. (a) 43. (b)

44. Match the following

	List -1	List-2
(a)	CLRI	1) Hyderabad
(b)	SENDOC	2) New Delhi
(c)	NASSDOC	3) Mumbai
(d)	BARC	4) Chennai

Codes:

	a	b	c	d
(A)	2	1	4	3
(B)	4	3	1	2
(C)	4	1	2	3
(D)	3	1	4	2

45. Match the following

	List -1	List-2
(a)	Fumigation	1) Acquisition
(b)	Building library collection	2) Preservation
(c)	Kardex	3) Reference service
(d)	Information desk	4) Registration of periodicals

Codes:

	a	b	c	d
(A)	1	2	3	4
(B)	2	3	1	4
(C)	3	2	4	1
(D)	4	3	2	1

Answer : 44. (c) 45. (d)

UGC –NATIONAL ELIGIBILITY TEST

Library & Information Science

Dec-2009

1. Who the quotation 'where is the wisdom, we lost in knowledge' is by
   (A) John Keats (B) M.P Karter
   (C) T.S Eliot (D) Marshall McLuhan
2. Entropy is a measure of?
   (A) Degree of relevance of information
   (B) Quantity of irrelevant information
   (C) Degree of uncertainty on information
   (D) Degree of certainty in information
3. CONPLIS (Indi(a) was set up in
   (A) 1985 (B) 1986
   (C) 1987 (D) 1988
4. First time effort for the development of libraries in India were made
   (A) S.R Ranganathan
   (B) S.Radhakrishnan
   (C) Siyaji Rao Gaekwad 1
   (D) Siyaji Rao Gaekwad 11
5. An e-book which doesn't require an internet connection to access its contents is
   (A) Web book (B) Palm book
   (C) Electronic ink book (D) Digital book

Answer : 1. (c) 2. (c) 3. (a) 4. (d) 5. (d)

6. Emerald full text database is published from
   (A) USA (B) Germany
   (C) France (D) UK
7. Who produced 'conservative, modern liberal theories of reference service'?
   (A) William A Katz (B) S.R Ranganathan
   (C) James I Wyer (D) R Emery
8. The input centre of INIS in India is
   (A) DRDO (B) DSIR
   (C) TROR (D) BARC
9. The provision of phase relations in DDC was made available from
   (A) 14th edition (B) 12th edition
   (C) 7th edition (D) 11th edition
10. RDA stands for
    (A) Resource Description Agency
    (B) Reference Description Access
    (C) Reference Description Agency
    (D) Resource Description and Access
11. Cost benefit analysis means
    (A) Value for money
    (B) Performance evaluation based on cost
    (C) Finding out unit cost
    (D) Performance evaluation based on inputs
12. Which national agency in India is assigning ISBN?
    (A) Raja Ram MohunRoy National Education Centre
    (B) Delhi public library
    (C) Federation of publishers in India
    (D) National library of India

Answer : 6. (d) 7. (b) 8. (d) 9. (d) 10. (d) 11. (b) 12. (a)

13. The term 'cyberspace was fist used by
    (A) Andrew Pollock (B) William Gibson
    (C) John Postal (D) Joe flower
14. RFID technology is used in
    (A) Acquisition (B) Serial control
    (C) Circulation (D) OPAC
15. The Boolean operator 'AND' is related to
    (A) Productive (B) Additive
    (C) Logical difference (D) None of the above
16. The process of configuring the disks into tracks and sectors is called
    (A) Booting (B) Formatting
    (C) Labeling (D) All the above
17. A research design is
    (A) A series of guide posts
    (B) A series of sampling
    (C) A hypothetical statement
    (D) A controller of variant
18. In a questionnaire on age, income and gender are the examples of
    (A) Dependent variable
    (B) Intervening variables
    (C) Independent variables
    (D) Manipulation variables
19. The simple Dubline Core Metadata Element set (DCMES) consists of
    (A) 10 elements (B) 12 elements
    (C) 14 elements (D) 15 elements

Answer : 13. (b) 14. (c) 15. (b) 16. (a) 17. (a) 18. (c) 19. (b)

20. 'Libraries as gateway to knowledge' is the title of the document
    (A) National information plicy, 1986
    (B) Information Technology Act, 2000
    (C) National Knowledge Commission on libraries, 2007
    (D) None of the above

21. Assertion (A) : INDEST conceive J-Gate as a customized gate for e-journals subscribed by the member libraries
    Reason (R) : J-gate provides a common access platform for all its members to search and share resources subscribed by the member libraries.
    (A) Both A and R are true, and R is the correct explanation
    (B) Both A and R are true, but R is not correct explanation
    (C) A is true, but R is false
    (D) A is false, R is true

22. Assertion (A): XML just like HTML is a meta language that is capable of containing extendable elements
    Reason (R) : XML develop and deploy new specific mark up enabling automatic authoring and processing of networked information.
    (A) A is false, but R is true
    (B) Both A and R are true and R is not the correct explanation
    (C) A is true, but R is false
    (D) Both A and R are true.

Answer : 20. (c) 21. (a) 22. (b)

23\. Assertion ((A) : Measuring the internet and in particular the web is a difficult task

Reason (R) : Web is considered as a new publishing medium with inadequate editorial process.

(A) A is false, but R is true
(B) Both A and R are true and R is not the correct explanation
(C) A is true, but R is false
(D) Both A and R are true.

24\. Assertion (A) : An indexing language is an artificial language as it uses controlled vocabulary.

Reason (R) : It provides different relationship between terms.

(A) Both A and R are false
(B) Both A and R are false
(C) A is true, but R is false
(D) A is false, but R is true.

25\. Assertion (A) : With large collection of documents, recall can be measured properly

Reason (R) : The proper estimation of maximum recall for a query requires detailed knowledge of all the documents in the collection.

(A) A is false, but R is true
(B) Both A and R are true and R is not the correct explanation
(C) A is true, but R is false
(D) Both A and R are true.

Answer : 23. (a) 24. (b) 25. (d)

26. Assertion (A) : In contemporary digital environment, IPR become the focal point

    Reason (R) : Many fold increase of unfair use of IP.

    (A) A and R are true

    (B) A and R are false

    (C) A is true and R is false

    (D) A is false but R is true

27. Assertion (A) : Library automation is at a slow pace in Indian libraries

    Reason (R) : Lack of UGC support lead to this situation.

    (A) Both A and R are true

    (B) Both A and R are false

    (C) A is true but R is false

    (D) A is false but R is true

28. Assertion (A) : The development of institutional repositories in India is at a slow pace

    Reason (R) : This can be attributed to the non availability of open source software and lack of interest among the LIS professionals.

    (A) Both A and R are true

    (B) Both A and R are false

    (C) A is true but R is false

    (D) A is false but R is true

Answer : 26. (c) 27. (c) 28. (c)

29. Assertion (A) : Subject gateway offer the user an alternative to 'Vacuum, cleaner' type of search engines. Such as Google, info seek, AltaVista etc.

    Reason (R) : Subject gateway hold manually created records. Rich resource description containing relevant information

    (A) Both A and R are true

    (B) Both A and R are true and R is not correct explanation

    (C) A is true but R is false

    (D) A is false but R is true

30. Assertion (A) : Para-professional staff supports the professional staff in library routines.

    Reason (R) : Para-professional staff acquires skill by experience.

    (A) A is false but R is true

    (B) A is true but R is false

    (C) Both A and R are false

    (D) Both A and R are false

31. Public library law has already been passed in the following states. Identify the correct chronological order in which they were enacted

    1) Uttaranchal 2) Orisa

    3) Gujarat 4) Hariyana

    (A) 1,2,3,4 (B) 4,2,3,1

    (C) 2,3,4,1 (D) 3,2,1,4

Answer : 29. (d) 30. (d) 31. (b)

32. Arrange in the chronological order the following persons who were associated with computing history.

1) J.Presper Eckart
2) John W Mauchly
3) August Ada
4) Charles Babbage

(A) 3,2,1,4
(B) 2,1,3,4
(C) 1,4,3,2
(D) 4,3,2,1

33. Arrange the following events of public library movement in chronological order.

1) Enactment of press and registration of Books act
2) Establishment of Punjab library, Lahore
3) Constitution of Fyzee committee
4) Declaration of imperial library as National library of India

(A) 1,3,4,2
(B) 1,2,3,4
(C) 2,3,4,1
(D) 4,1,3,2

34. Arrange the following layers of OSI model in the sequence in which they function

1) Network layer
2) Physical layer
3) Transport layer
4) Data link layer

(A) 3,4,2,1
(B) 4,2,1,3
(C) 2,4,1,3
(D) 1,2,3,4

35. Arrange the following four quadrants of spiral of scientific method in their logical order.

1) Ascendant
2) Nadir
3) Zenith
4) Descendent

(A) 4,1,3,2
(B) 1,3,4,2
(C) 3,2,1,4
(D) 2,1,3,4

Answer : 32. (d) 33. (b) 34. (c) 35. (c)

36. Arrange the following in order of their publication
    1) Classified Catalogue Code
    2) Prolegomena to library classification
    3) Five laws of library science
    4) Colon Classification

    (A) 1,4,3,2 (B) 3,2,4,1
    (C) 3,4,1,2 (D) 4,1,2,3

37. Arrange the following bibliographies according to their date origin
    1) Indian National Bibliography
    2) Cumulative book index
    3) Books in print
    4) British National bibliography

    (A) 3,4,1,2 (B) 2,3,4,1
    (C) 1,2,3,4 (D) 4,2,1,3

38. Arrange the following schemes of classification according to their year of origin
    1) Colon Classification
    2) Expansive Classification
    3) Universal Decimal Classification
    4) Dewey Decimal Classification

    (A) 2,3,4,1 (B) 3,4,1,2
    (C) 4,2,3,1 (D) 1,2,3,4

39. Arrange the following principles and canons according to their levels as enunciated by Dr.S.R Ranganathan
    1) Principles of cataloguing
    2) General Normative principles
    3) Laws of library science
    4) Canons of Cataloguing

    (A) 1,4,3,2 (B) 2,3,4,1
    (C) 2,1,4,3 (D) 1,4,2,3

Answer : 36. (c) 37. (a) 38. (c) 39. (b)

40. Arrange the following Associations according to their year of formation

1) ASLIB	2) LA
3) ALA	4) SLA
(A) 3,2,4,1	(B) 2,4,1,3
(C) 3,1,4,2	(D) 4,1,3,2

41. Match the following

	List -1	**List-2**
(a)	Little science, Big science	1) S.C Bradfold
(b)	Documentation	2) William Martin
(c)	The third wave	3) Enic Jde solla price
(d)	Information society	4) F.W Taylor

Codes:

	a	b	c	d
(A)	1	2	3	4
(B)	3	1	4	2
(C)	4	3	2	1
(D)	2	1	4	3

42. Match the following

	List -1	**List-2**
(a)	Keyword Indexing	1) J.R Sharp
(b)	Citation Indexing	2) H.P Luhn
(c)	Uniterm Indexing	3) E.Garfield
(d)	SLIC Indexing	4) M.Taub

Codes:

	a	b	c	d
(A)	2	3	4	1
(B)	3	4	1	2
(C)	4	1	3	2
(D)	1	3	2	4

Answer : 40. (a) 41. (d) 42. (a)

43. Match the following

	List -1	**List-2**
(a)	Web Navigation Element	1) Tele communication
(b)	Shift + Tab	2) SQL
(c)	ANSI Standard	3) Hyperlink
(d)	TELNET	4) Select the previous link

Codes:

	a	b	c	d
(A)	1	2	3	4
(B)	4	3	2	1
(C)	3	4	2	1
(D)	2	3	1	4

44. Match the following

	List -1	**List-2**
(a)	Mcfee	1) DOAJ
(b)	Directory	2) Antivirus
(c)	Personal webpage	3) Vendor on the internet
(d)	Amazon.com	4) Blogs

Codes:

	a	b	c	d
(A)	2	1	4	3
(B)	1	4	3	2
(C)	2	3	4	1
(D)	4	3	2	1

Answer : 43. (c) 44. (a)

45. Match the following

	List -1	List-2
(a)	Theory of knowledge	1) Henry Fayaol
(b)	IS: 1553-1960	2) Metadata format
(c)	Resource sharing	3) Library Building
(d)	TEI	4) Epistemology

Codes:

	a	b	c	d
(A)	4	2	1	3
(B)	4	1	2	3
(C)	3	4	2	1
(D)	2	3	4	1

Answer : 45. (c)

UGC –NATIONAL ELIGIBILITY TEST

Library & Information Science

Dec-2008

1. Who is the chairman of National Knowledge Commission?
   (A) Harsha Paresh (B) P.B Mangla
   (C) Kalpana Das Gupta (D) Sam pitroda
2. Which is the primary source for finding out Indian periodicals in Agriculture?
   (A) Ulrich International Periodical directory
   (B) Reference Asia
   (C) Press in India
   (D) INFA year book
3. Which of the following indexes only papers presented in the conferences?
   (A) LISA
   (B) Current Research Abstract
   (C) Research in Progress
   (D) ISTP
4. Appropriate communication media for CD – Net is
   (A) Twisted wires (B) Optical fiber
   (C) Co-axial cables (D) Ethernet cables
5. IATLIS is an association of
   (A) Library science faculty
   (B) Special libraries
   (C) Libraries of public libraries
   (D) Librarians pf teacher's Training colleges

Answer : 1. (d) 2. (a) 3. (d) 4. (b) 5. (a)

6. Identify the association that has changed its original name

   (A) ILA (B) SLA

   (C) LA (D) ALA.

7. Recall and Precision rations are used in the evaluation of

   (A) Reference service

   (B) Information retrieval

   (C) Bibliographic service

   (D) Document delivery service

8. Number of digits in ISBN now is

   (A) 10 (B) 11

   (C) 12 (D) 13

9. 'Emerald' is a database of

   (A) Gems and jewelry literature

   (B) Material science literature

   (C) Library science literature

   (D) Earth science literature

10. TQM was promulgamated by

    (A) Deming and Juran (B) Maslow

    (C) Druker (D) Taylor

11. MESH is the name of

    (A) Medical library

    (B) Controlled Vocabulary

    (C) Online database

    (D) CSIR Unit

12. Rules for dictionary catalogue was devised by

    (A) A. Panizzi (B) C.C Jewet

    (C) S. Lubetzky (D) C.A Cutter

Answer : 6. (c) 7. (b) 8. (d) 9. (c) 10. (a) 11. (b) 12. (d)

13. A Gazette gives information about
    (A) Places of tourist interests
    (B) History of places
    (C) Official announcement and notification
    (D) Old records
14. Glossary is a
    (A) List of technical words with definitions
    (B) Lists of words in a language
    (C) List of thematically arranged words
    (D) Alphabetical index to passages of work
15. National library of blind and handicapped of India is located at
    (A) Madras (B) Tarjore
    (C) Dehradum (D) Delhi
16. The term 'information retrieval' was coined by
    (A) H.P Luhn (B) Calvin Moores
    (C) Mortomer Taub (D) Derek Austin
17. The term 'hypertext' was coined by
    (A) Vannever Bush (B) John Brown
    (C) M.C Kith (D) Ted Nelson
18. With which agency did UNESCO collaborate to establish UNISIST?
    (A) ICSU (B) FID
    (C) IFLA (D) ILA
19. Which University appointed the first full time University Librarian?
    (A) Delhi University (B) Punjab University
    (C) Madras University (D) Calcutta University

Answer : 13. (c) 14. (a) 15. (c) 16. (b) 17. (d) 18. (c) 19. (c)

20. Assertion (A): Classification and indexing have always been of central intellectual interest in IR

    Reason (R) : Conceptual analysis of content of queries and documents are essential input to an IR system.

    Codes:

    (A) A is true but R is false

    (B) A is false but R is true

    (C) A and R both are true

    (D) A and R both are partially true

21. Assertion (A) : Any change in the environment of the subject can not affect the state of the subject.

    Reason (R) : A subject can be viewed as a system consisting of a set of interacting component ideas.

    Codes:

    (A) A is true but R is false

    (B) A is false but R is true

    (C) A and R both are true

    (D) A and R both are false

Answer : 20. (d) 21. (b)

22. Assertion (A) : Action research is a form of interpretive research to study human actions and social practices for immediate application

Reason (R) : Action research is an applied research, which is focused on the solution to local problems, not to develop any theory fo general application.

Codes:

(A) A is true but R is false

(B) A is false but R is true

(C) A and R both are true

(D) A and R both are false

23. Assertion (A): Information system support promotion of research development and innovation relating to the national development of a country.

Reason (R) : Information is the basic input to the development.

Codes:

(A) Both A and R are true and R is not the correct explanation

(B) Both A and R are true and R is the correct explanation

(C) A is true but R is false

(D) A is false but R is true

Answer : 22. (d) 23. (b)

24. Assertion (A): Many projects and initiatives are taken to create digital libraries

    Reason (R) : Digital library improves the professional status of libraries.

    Codes:

    (A) Both A and R are true
    (B) Both A and R are false
    (C) A is true but R is false
    (D) A is false but R is true

25. Assertion (A): IFLA's UBC programme encourages the use and exchange of standardized bibliographic description.

    Reason (R) : Use of standard enables to bring uniformity in bibliographic description and interchange of bibliographic data.

    Codes:

    (A) Both A and R are false
    (B) Both A and R are true
    (C) R is true but A is false
    (D) A is true but R is false

26. Assertion (A): UNESCO championed the cause of public library movement.

    Reason (R) : UNESCO's concerns for public library movement is reflected in its public Library movement.

    Codes:

    (A) A is true but R is false
    (B) A is false but R is true
    (C) A and R both are false
    (D) A and R both are true

Answer : 24. (c) 25. (b) 26. (d)

27. Assertion (A) : PRECIS is not based upon any particular system of classification

Reason (R) : PRECIS is not built around any theoretical ideas on classification

Codes:

(A) A is true but R is false

(B) A is false but R is true

(C) A and R both are true

(D) A and R both are false

28. Arrange according to the year of establishment

(A) Chemical abstract, Biological abstract, Science citation index, Indian Science abstract

(B) Chemical abstract, Science citation index, Indian Science abstract, Biological abstract

(C) Biological abstract, Chemical abstract, Science citation index, Indian Science abstract

(D) Chemical abstract, Biological abstract, Indian Science abstract, Science Citation index.

29. The correct sequence of information flow is

(A) Message → source → channel → receiver

(B) Source → message → channel → receiver

(C) Message → channel → source → receiver

(D) Message → channel → receiver → source

30. Arrange the following classification schemes in the order of year of origin

(A) UDC, Expansive classification, DDC,CC

(B) Expansive classification, UDC, CC,DDC

(C) DDC, CC, Expansive classification, UDC

(D) DDC, Expansive classification, UDC, CC

Answer : 27. (a) 28. (a) 29. (b) 30. (d)

31. Arrange the following public Library Acts according to the year of enactment.
    (A) Manipur, West Bengal, Kerala, Mizoram
    (B) West Bengal, Manipur, Kerala, Mizoram
    (C) West Bengal, Kerala, Manipur, Mizoram
    (D) West Bengal, Manipur, Mizoram, Kerala.

32. Arrange the following associations according the year of establishment
    (A) ALA,CILIP(L(A), Special library association , ASLIB
    (B) CILIP (L(A), ALA, Special library association, ASLIB
    (C) ALA, Special library association, CILIP (L(A), ASLIB
    (D) ASLIB, ALA, CILIP (L(A), Special library association

33. Arrange the following standards according to the year of their introduction
    (A) ISBN, ICCP, CCF, ISDS
    (B) CCF, ICCP, ISBN, ISDS
    (C) ICCP, ISBN, ISDS, CCF
    (D) ISBD, ISBN, ICCP, CCF

Answer : 31. (b) 32. (a) 33. (c)

34. Match the following

	List -1	List-2
(a)	Principles of librarianship	1) Berwick Sayers
(b)	Practical guide for classification	2) S.R Ranganathan
(c)	Rules for dictionary catalogue	3) D.J Urquart
(d)	Five laws of library science	4) C.A Cutter

Codes:

	a	b	c	d
(A)	3	1	4	2
(B)	1	2	3	4
(C)	3	2	4	1
(D)	1	3	4	2

35. Match the following

	List -1	List-2
(a)	Informatique	1) English
(b)	Informatik	2) Italian
(c)	Informatica	3) French
(d)	Informatics	4) German

Codes:

	a	b	c	d
(A)	3	4	2	1
(B)	2	1	4	3
(C)	4	3	1	2
(D)	3	1	2	4

Answer : 34. (a) 35. (a)

36. Match the following

	List -1	List-2
(a)	Bibliographic description	1) Current awareness service
(b)	Short range reference service	2) Post coordinate indexing
(c)	SDI	3) Abstract
(d)	Uniterm	4) Ready reference source

Codes:

	a	b	c	d
(A)	3	4	1	2
(B)	2	1	3	4
(C)	4	1	2	3
(D)	2	3	4	1

37. Arrange the following according to their increasing storage capacity

1) Cartridge
2) CD-ROM
3) Floppy Disk
4) DVD

(A) 3,1,2,4
(B) 1,2,3,4
(C) 4,3,1,2
(D) 1,3,2,4

38. Match the following

	List -1	List-2
(a)	DDC 19th edition	1) John Camaroni
(b)	DDC 20th edition	2) MS Mitchel
(c)	DDC 21st edition	3) John Mitchell
(d)	DDC 22nd edition	4) Benjamin Custer

Codes:

	a	b	c	d
(A)	2	4	3	1
(B)	2	1	4	3
(C)	2	4	1	3
(D)	4	1	2	3

Answer : 36. (a) 37. (d) 38. (d)

39. Match the following

	List-1	**List-2**
(a)	Nascent micro thought	1) Colon Classification
(b)	Access Point	2) Motivation
(c)	Physiological needs	3) Documentation
(d)	Analytic-Synthetic classification	4) AACR-II

Codes:

	a	b	c	d
(A)	3	4	2	1
(B)	3	2	1	4
(C)	2	1	4	3
(D)	1	2	3	4

40. Match the following

	List-1	**List-2**
(a)	SHE	1) Nuclear energy
(b)	MESH	2) Education
(c)	ERIC	3) Medicine
(d)	INIS	4) Engineering

Codes:

	a	b	c	d
(A)	1	3	2	4
(B)	4	3	2	1
(C)	2	3	1	4
(D)	1	2	3	4

Answer : 39. (a) 40. (b)

41. Match the following

	List-1	List-2
(a)	Five laws of library science	1) C.D Needham
(b)	Subject approach to information	2) S.R Ranganathan
(c)	Organizing knowledge in libraries	3) B.C Vickery and A. Vickery
(d)	Information science in theory & practice	4) AACR-II

Codes:

	a	b	c	d
(A)	2	4	1	3
(B)	1	3	4	2
(C)	3	2	4	1
(D)	4	2	3	1

42. Match the following

	List-1	List-2
(a)	Melvil Dewey	1) Belgium
(b)	Berwick Sayers	2) USA
(c)	B.S Kesavan	3) Britain
(d)	Paul Otlet	4) India

Codes:

	a	b	c	d
(A)	2	4	1	3
(B)	4	3	1	2
(C)	2	3	4	1
(D)	2	1	3	4

Answer : 41. (a) 42. (c)

43. Match the following

	List-1	List-2
(a)	UBC	1) FID
(b)	UDC	2) IFLA
(c)	MARC	3) ASTINFO
(d)	Document supply system	4) Library of Congress

Codes:

	a	b	c	d
(A)	2	4	1	3
(B)	2	1	4	3
(C)	1	2	3	4
(D)	3	2	4	1

44. Match the following

	List-1	List-2
(a)	Bradford's law	1) Author's production
(b)	Lotka's law	2) Citation indexing
(c)	Eugene Garfield	3) Word frequency
(d)	Zip's law	4) Scattering

Codes:

	a	b	c	d
(A)	1	2	4	3
(B)	3	4	2	1
(C)	4	2	1	3
(D)	4	1	2	3

Answer : 43. (b) 44. (d)

45. Match the following

	List-1	List-2
(a)	Mission oriented	1) Patent Information system
(b)	Social Science Oriented	2) DESIDOC
(c)	Science Subject Oriented	3) NISSAT
(d)	Material Oriented	4) NASSDOC

Codes:

	a	b	c	d
(A)	3	4	2	1
(B)	4	3	2	1
(C)	1	2	3	4
(D)	2	3	4	1

Answer : 45. (a)

UGC –NATIONAL ELIGIBILITY TEST

Library & Information Science

June-2008

1. Who is the chairman of National Knowledge Commission?
   (A) Dr. Sukhadeo Thorat
   (B) Dr.M.S Swami Nathan
   (C) Dr.Bakachandra Mungekar
   (D) Sam pitroda
2. Who has not changed its name?
   (A) Library Association, UK
   (B) ALA
   (C) ASLIB
   (D) IFLA
3. Which of the following is not correct?
   (A) Malsow's need analysis is useful for understanding motivation of employees.
   (B) Theory Z is the contribution of Japanese style of Management
   (C) Money is the most powerful motivating agent
   (D) Mission of an organization is essentially abstract
4. NISCAIRE is a part of
   (A) DST (B) ISRO
   (C) DSIR (D) CSIR

Answer : 1. (d) 2. (b) 3. (c) 4. (d)

5. Use of microfilming is considerably reduced due to
   (A) Problem of preservation of microfilms
   (B) Need for use microfilm reader
   (C) Availability of better technology in the form of digitalization
   (D) High cost involved in it.
6. Opaque paper is a
   (A) Ultra-white paper
   (B) Ultra-white thin paper
   (C) Transparent paper
   (D) Non-transparent paper
7. Which of the following is a public domain database?
   (A) INIS (B) AGRIS
   (C) Chemical Abstract (D) MEDLINE
8. In which library service barcode technology is used
   (A) Stock verification (B) Library security
   (C) Circulation (D) Reference service
9. One of the following journals is published in UK
   (A) Library Quarterly
   (B) Program
   (C) Libri
   (D) Herald of Library science
10. 'Fair Use' is a term most relevant to
    (A) Intellectual property rights
    (B) Books borrowed for home reading
    (C) Copyright
    (D) Use of reference books

Answer : 5. (a) 6. (a) 7. (b) 8. (c) 9. (b) 10. (a)

11. Which of the following does not fall into the category of pre-coordinate indexing?
    (A) Chain Indexing
    (B) Uniform Indexing
    (C) LCSH
    (D) Sear's list of subject headings
12. Dublin Core is
    (A) A set of core activities of a National library
    (B) Collection of Metadata elements
    (C) Network for the city of Dublin
    (D) Revised version of MARC
13. 'Best is the enemy of Good' is said by
    (A) Drury (B) Urquarts
    (C) Foskett (D) Shera
14. Which of the following is not associated with communication system?
    (A) Receiver (B) Sender
    (C) Channel (D) Entropy
15. One of the following is not open source software
    (A) D'space (B) Windows
    (C) Green stone (D) Linux
16. DESIDOC is documentation centre for
    (A) Indigenous knowledge
    (B) Defence science
    (C) Rural development
    (D) Khadi and village industries
17. Questionnaire is a
    (A) Research method
    (B) Measurement technique
    (C) Tool for data collection
    (D) All the above

Answer : 11. (b) 12. (b) 13. (b) 14. (d) 15. (b) 16. (b) 17. (c)

18. Mean, Median and Mode are
    (A) Measures of deviation
    (B) Ways of sampling
    (C) Measures of central tendency
    (D) None of the above
19. 'Cranfield studies' are example of
    (A) Survey research
    (B) Experimental research
    (C) Historical research
    (D) Case study
20. Assertion (A): As the level of recall increases, precision tends to decrease.

    Reason (R) : Recall and precision tend to vary inversely.

    Codes:
    (A) Both A and R are true
    (B) A is true but R is false
    (C) Both are partially true
    (D) A and R both are false
21. Assertion (A): Operators using AND, OR and NOT are mostly used in online information retrieval.

    Reason (R) : User interfaces cannot transform the natural language input into Boolean search query.

    Codes:
    (A) Both A and R are true
    (B) A is true but R is false
    (C) R is true but A is false
    (D) Both A and R are false

Answer : 18. (c) 19. (b) 20. (a) 21. (c)

22. Assertion (A): Maximization of the use of documents is the motto of library

    Reason (R) : Maximization of the use of documents in the library satisfies the 5th law of library science.

    Codes:

    (A) Both A and R are true

    (B) Both A and R are false

    (C) A is true but R is false

    (D) R is true but A is false

23. Assertion (A): User profile is an essential component of SDI service

    Reason (R) : SDI is a personalized current awareness service.

    Codes:

    (A) Both A and R are true

    (B) Both A and R are false

    (C) Both A and R are partially true

    (D) A is true but R is false

24. Assertion (A): AACR-II like CCC can satisfy the all approaches of users

    Reason (R) : Both AACR-II and CCC are comprehensive cataloguing codes.

    Codes:

    (A) A is true but R is false

    (B) R is true but A is false

    (C) Both A and R are true

    (D) Both A and R are false

Answer : 22. (c) 23. (a) 24. (c)

25. Assertion (A): document transfer and information transfer are not the same

    Reason (R) : Assimilation of content of the document by the user constitutes information transfer.

    Codes:

    (A) A is true but R is false

    (B) R is true but A is false

    (C) Both A and R are true

    (D) Both A and R are false

26. Assertion (A): ISO 9000 is a quality framework which calls dor documentation to adopt TQM in library.

    Reason (R) : ISO 9000 is a valuable component of TQM.

    Codes:

    (A) A is true but R is false

    (B) R is true but A is false

    (C) Both A and R are false

    (D) Both A and R are true

27. Assertion (A): Consortia cannot provide an effective strategy to increase the buying power of individual libraries.

    Reason (R) : Consortia arrangement saves the funds of the libraries in developing their information sources.

    Codes:

    (A) A is false but R is true

    (B) A is true but R is false

    (C) Both A and R are false

    (D) Both A and R are true

Answer : 25. (a) 26. (d) 27. (a)

28. Arrange the following in the order of computer generations

    1) Integrated circuits 2) Transistor
    3) Vacuum tube 4) Chip

    Codes:

    (A) 4,2,3,1 (B) 3,2,1,4
    (C) 1,2,3,4 (D) 3,4,2,1

29. Match the following

	List -1	**List-2**
(a)	BLAISE project	1) Library of Congress
(b)	MARC project	2) Intel
(c)	Union catalogue project	3) INSDOC
(d)	Microchip	4) British library

Codes:

	a	b	c	d
(A)	3	2	4	1
(B)	1	2	3	4
(C)	4	1	3	2
(D)	2	3	1	4

30. Which is the correct logical sequence of the following?

    (A) Information, Knowledge, data, wisdom
    (B) Knowledge, information, Wisdom data
    (C) Data, knowledge, Information, wisdom
    (D) Data, Information. Knowledge wisdom

Answer : 28. (b) 29. (c) 30. (d)

31. Subject indexing systems were developed in the order as
    (A) Chain indexing, systematic indexing, PRECIS, COMPASS
    (B) Systematic indexing, Chain indexing, PRECIS, COMPASS
    (C) Systematic indexing, PRECIS, Chain indexing COMPASS
    (D) Systematic indexing, COMPASS, Chain indexing, PRECIS

32. Arrange the following associations in the order of year of establishment
    (A) SIS, IASLIC, IATLIS, ILA
    (B) IASLIC, ILA, SIS, IATLIS
    (C) ILA, SIS, IASLIC, IATLIS
    (D) IALA, IASLIC, IATLIS, SIS

33. Arrange the following Act according to year of enactment.
    (A) Copyright Act, The patent Act, IT Act, IPR Act
    (B) The patent Act, Copyright Act, , IT Act, IPR Act
    (C) Copyright Act, IPR Act The patent Act, IT Act
    (D) Copyright Act, The patent Act, IPR Act IT Act

Answer : 31. (b) 32. (d) 33. (d)

34. Arrange the different codes according to year of origin

    (A) Anthony pannizi code, Cutter's rules for dictionary catalogue, Classified Catalogue code, Anglo American cat. rules-II

    (B) Anthony pannizi code, classified catalogue code, Cutter's rules for dictionary Catalogue, Anglo American cat. Rules-II

    (C) Anthony pannizi code, Anglo American cat. rules-II , Classified catalogue code Cutter's rules for dictionary catalogue, ,

    (D) Anthony pannizi code, Cutter's rules for dictionary catalogue,, Anglo American cat. Rules-II, Classified catalogue code

35. Arrange the following according to the year of publication

    (A) Encyclopaedia Britannica, Encyclopaedia Americana, Encyclopedia of Library science, Mc GrawHill encyclopedia of science and technology.

    (B) Encyclopaedia Britannica, Encyclopedia of Library science, Mc GrawHill encyclopedia of science and technology, Encyclopaedia Americana.

    (C) Encyclopaedia Britannica, Encyclopaedia Americana, Mc GrawHill encyclopedia of science and technology Encyclopedia of Library science.

    (D) Encyclopaedia Britannica, Mc GrawHill encyclopedia of science and technology, Encyclopaedia Americana, Encyclopedia of Library science.

Answer : 34. (a) 35. (c)

36. Match the following

	List -1	**List-2**
(a)	Conventional	1) Patents
(b)	New-conventional	2) Printed books
(c)	Non-conventional	3)Satellite imageries
(d)	Meta documents	4) Audio- visual materials

Codes:

	a	b	c	d
(A)	1	2	3	4
(B)	2	1	4	3
(C)	4	1	3	2
(D)	3	2	1	4

37. Match the following

	List -1	**List-2**
(a)	Library is people's university	1) Kothari
(b)	Library is a growing organism	2) Urquart
(c)	Library can be useful to society	3) Ranganathan
(d)	Library is the heart of the university	4) Sayajiraho Gayakward

Codes:

	a	b	c	d
(A)	4	3	2	1
(B)	4	1	3	2
(C)	2	4	3	1
(D)	4	2	1	3

Answer : 36. (b) 37. (a)

38. Match the following

	List -1	List-2
(a)	P. Wasserman	1) Line of thinking
(b)	P. Atherton	2) Foundation of education for librarianship
(c)	J.H Shera	3) New librarianship
(d)	Maurice B line	4) Putting knowledge to work

Codes:

	a	b	c	d
(A)	1	2	3	4
(B)	2	1	3	4
(C)	4	3	1	2
(D)	3	4	2	1

39. Match the following

	List -1	List-2
(a)	Theory of X and Y	1) Frederic Taylor
(b)	Scientific management	2) Ouchi
(c)	Need hierarchy	3) A. Maslow
(d)	Theory Z	4) D.Mc Grager

Codes:

	a	b	c	d
(A)	3	2	1	4
(B)	4	3	2	1
(C)	2	1	4	3
(D)	4	1	3	2

Answer : 38. (d) 39. (d)

40. Match the following

	List -1	**List-2**
(a)	UDC	1) H.E Bliss
(b)	DDC	2) C.A Cutter
(c)	Expansive classification	3) Otlat and La Fontane
(d)	Bibliographic classification	4) M. Dewey

Codes:

	a	b	c	d
(A)	3	1	2	4
(B)	3	4	2	1
(C)	3	2	4	1
(D)	1	2	3	4

41. Match the following

	List -1	**List-2**
(a)	British Library	1) Russia
(b)	Bibliotheque National	2) USA
(c)	Lenin Library	3) UK
(d)	Library of Congress	4) France

Codes:

	a	b	c	d
(A)	4	3	1	2
(B)	1	2	3	4
(C)	3	4	1	2
(D)	3	4	2	1

Answer : 40. (b) 41. (c)

42. Match the following

	List -1		**List-2**
(a)	Windows	1)	A revolving disc on which data is stored
(b)	Microprocessor	2)	It is used for processing of text
(c)	Word processor	3)	Collection of programmes for computer System
(d)	Software	4)	A graphical user interface working as DOS

Codes:

	a	b	c	d
(A)	4	1	2	3
(B)	3	2	1	4
(C)	2	3	4	1
(D)	1	2	3	4

43. Match the following

	List -1	**List-2**
(a)	Orissa library act	1) 2006
(b)	Goa library act	2) 2005
(c)	Uttaranchal library act	3) 2001
(d)	Uttar Pradesh library act	4) 1994

Codes:

	a	b	c	d
(A)	1	2	3	4
(B)	3	4	2	1
(C)	4	3	2	1
(D)	2	1	3	4

Answer : 42. (a) 43. (b)

44. Match the following

	List -1	List-2
(a)	Software	1) Key board
(b)	Hardware	2) CD
(c)	Storage devise	3) SOUL
(d)	I/O Devise	4) CPU

Codes:

	a	b	c	d
(A)	2	4	3	1
(B)	2	3	4	1
(C)	3	2	4	1
(D)	3	4	2	1

45. Match the following

	List -1	List-2
(a)	Planning	1) Delegation of authority
(b)	Staffing	2) Audit
(c)	Control	3) Promotion
(d)	Organizing	4) Resource management

Codes:

	a	b	c	d
(A)	1	2	3	4
(B)	2	4	1	3
(C)	3	1	2	4
(D)	4	3	2	1

Answer : 44. (d) 45. (d)

SPC	Stored Program Control
SPIN	[illegible] Interest Network
SQL	Structured Query Language
SSCI	Social Science Citation Index
STAIRS	Storage & information retrieval system